NUMBER® CORNER

SECOND EDITION
STUDENT BOOK

GRADE
5

Published by The MATH LEARNING CENTER Salem, Oregon

Number Corner Second Edition Grade 5 Student Book

The Number Corner Grade 5 package consists of:

Number Corner Grade 5 Teachers Guide Volumes 1–3

Number Corner Grade 5 Teacher Masters

Number Corner Grade 5 Student Book

Number Corner Grade 5 Teacher Masters Answer Key

Number Corner Grade 5 Student Book Answer Key

Number Corner Grade 5 Components & Manipulatives

Assessment Guide:

• Number Corner Assessments

• Comprehensive Growth Assessment

Digital resources noted in italics.

The Math Learning Center, PO Box 12929, Salem, Oregon 97309. Tel 1 (800) 575-8130
www.mathlearningcenter.org

Prepared for publication using Mac OS X and Adobe Creative Suite.
Printed in the United States of America.

To reorder this book, refer to number 2NC5SB5 (package of 5).

QBN5901
06012020_LSC
Updated 2017-06-27.

Bridges in Mathematics is a standards-based K–5 curriculum that provides a unique blend of concept development and skills practice in the context of problem solving. It incorporates Number Corner, a collection of daily skill-building activities for students.

The Math Learning Center is a nonprofit organization serving the education community. Our mission is to inspire and enable individuals to discover and develop their mathematical confidence and ability. We offer innovative and standards-based professional development, curriculum, materials, and resources to support learning and teaching. To find out more, visit us at www.mathlearningcenter.org.

ISBN 978-1-60262-456-6

Number Corner Grade 5
Student Book

Problem String Work Space begins on page A1 at
the back of the Number Corner Student Book.

NAME | **DATE**

 ## What's Missing?

1 Raj's class is collecting information about prisms they are building, but he is missing some of the data. Fill in the missing information in the table below.

Building Prisms				
Dimensions of the Base	**Area of the Base**	**Number of Layers**	**Volume**	**Dimensions of the Prism**
4×2		2		
		2		$(3 \times 3) \times 2$
2×10			40 cubic units	
$4 \times \underline{}$	36 sq. units	3		
5×2			100 cubic units	
	35 sq. units			$(5 \times 7) \times 4$
6×5		8		
$\underline{} \times 5$	25 sq. units	4		
		3		$(2 \times 9) \times 3$
				$(2 \times 7) \times 4$

2 Help Raj and his partner fill in the blanks in the equations below.

a $(4 \times 3) \times 6 = (2 \times 3) \times \underline{}$

b $9 \times (6 \times 6) = 9 \times (\underline{} \times 3)$

c $(3 \times 4) \times 6 = 24 \times \underline{}$

3 Raj and his partner disagree about the following equations. Tell whether each is true or false.

a $(5 \times 2) \times 4 = 2 \times (4 \times 5)$ \underline{}

b $8 \times (10 \times 2) = 16 \times (5 \times 1)$ \underline{}

c $2 \times (9 \times 3) = 3 \times 18$ \underline{}

Multiple Game Board

Player 1 _____   Player 2 _____

2	3	4	5	6	7	8
9	10	11	12	13	14	15
16	17	18	19	20	21	22
23	24	25	26	27	28	29
30	31	32	33	34	35	36
37	38	39	40	41	42	43
44	45	46	47	48	49	50

Player 1 Total _____   Player 2 Total _____

NAME _____ **| DATE** _____

⊞ Maddy's Multiples

1 Maddy is playing the Multiple Game. She goes first. She chooses the number 36.

a How many points does Maddy get? _____

b How many points does Maddy's partner get? _____

c Was 36 a good choice for Maddy's first turn? Explain.

Multiple Game Board						
2	3	4	5	6	7	8
9	10	11	12	13	14	15
16	17	18	19	20	21	22
23	24	25	26	27	28	29
30	31	32	33	34	35	36
37	38	39	40	41	42	43
44	45	46	47	48	49	50

2 List the factors for each number below. Write P next to numbers that are prime and C next to numbers that are composite.

	29	
	24	

	25	
	23	

3 Which of the four numbers in problem 2 would you choose if you were going first in the Multiple Game? Why?

4 List the factors each pair of numbers below has in common.

ex What factors do 24 and 36 have in common? <u>2, 3, 4, 6, 12</u>

a What factors do 20 and 28 have in common? _____

b What factors do 18 and 32 have in common? _____

5 List two multiples that each pair of numbers below has in common.

ex What are 2 multiples that 6 and 12 have in common? <u>12, 24</u>

a What are 2 multiples that 3 and 5 have in common? _____

b What are 2 multiples that 4 and 7 have in common? _____

3

Rock Hopping page 1 of 2

Use the blank space to solve each problem. Show all your work including numbers, words, or labeled sketches. Write a complete sentence below your work to show the answer.

1 Two frogs, DJ and Freddy, were hopping from rock to rock in their favorite stream. In all, there were 36 rocks in the stream. DJ landed on every second rock and Freddy landed on every third rock. Which rocks did they *both* land on?

2 A new friend, Sue, joined in and landed on every 6th rock. Which rocks did all three frogs land on?

NAME _____ | **DATE** _____

Rock Hopping page 2 of 2

3 If the three friends keep jumping:

a Will DJ land on the 51st rock? How do you know?

b Will Freddy land on the 51st rock? How do you know?

c What is the first rock that all three frogs will land on after the 51st rock? How do you know?

Field Trip Snacks page 1 of 2

Use the blank space to solve each problem. Show all your work including numbers, words, or labeled sketches. Write a complete sentence below your work to show the answer.

1 A parent donated 36 fruit cups and 24 bananas to the fifth grade. The teacher wanted to make field trip snack bags with the donated food and wondered about the ways that the snacks could be packed. To be fair, the teacher wants to makes sure that all the bags are exactly the same.

a What is the greatest number of snack bags that the teacher can make, if each bag is identical? How do you know?

b What other numbers of snack bags could she make? How do you know?

Field Trip Snacks page 2 of 2

2 Another parent also donated 24 bananas, so there are 48 bananas total. Now what is the greatest number of snack bags that can be made?

3 The teacher realized that she miscounted and had only 30 fruit cups. How many snack bags can she make with 48 bananas and 30 fruit cups?

4 What do the different numbers of snack bags that can be made have to do with the number of fruit cups and number of bananas?

Thinking About Volume page 1 of 2

One measure of a three-dimensional figure is its volume. The volume of a solid figure is the number of cubes of a given size it takes to build that figure. Volume is measured in cubic units, or cubes.

1 Build this figure and then find its volume. Label the volume as *cubic units*.

2 One way you can find the volume of a figure is to count the cubes one by one. A more efficient way to find the volume of a figure is to look for groups of cubes that can be added together. Find two different ways (that don't involve counting the cubes one by one) to determine the volume of the buildings in each pair below. Use loops or arrows to show your groups and write an equation to represent your work. Be sure to label each total as *cubic units*.

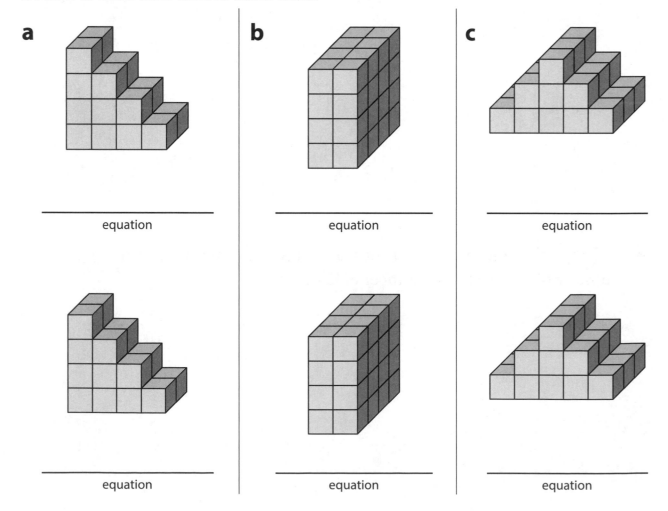

a

_____
equation

b

_____
equation

c

_____
equation

_____
equation

_____
equation

_____
equation

Thinking About Volume page 2 of 2

3 Gabby and her little sister, Elena, were making cube buildings. One of the buildings Gabby made had a 3 × 4 base and was 2 layers tall. Elena added a tower on top of Gabby's building that had a 2 × 2 base and was 3 layers tall. What was the volume of the sisters' building? Show all your work.

Views & Volume page 1 of 2

Top View	Right Side View	Front View	
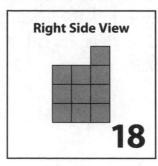 **17**	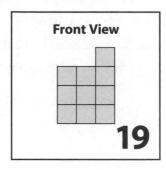 **18**	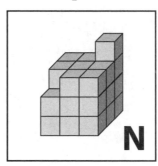 **19**	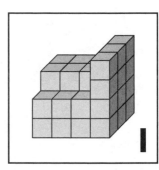 **?**

1 Circle the marker that should come next in the sequence above.

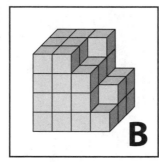 **G**	**B**	**N**	**I**

2 How did you figure it out? Use labeled sketches, words, or numbers to explain. (You can use your cubes to help if you want.)

10

NAME _____ | DATE _____

Views & Volume page 2 of 2

3 Find the volume of each solid figure shown below, using a method other than counting the cubes one by one. For each figure, use loops and an equation to show your method. Don't forget to label your answers as cubic units.

a

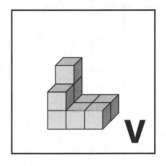

volume: _____

b

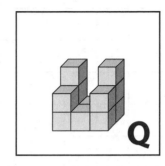

volume: _____

c

volume: _____

d

volume: _____

Carrot Masses Double Line Graph

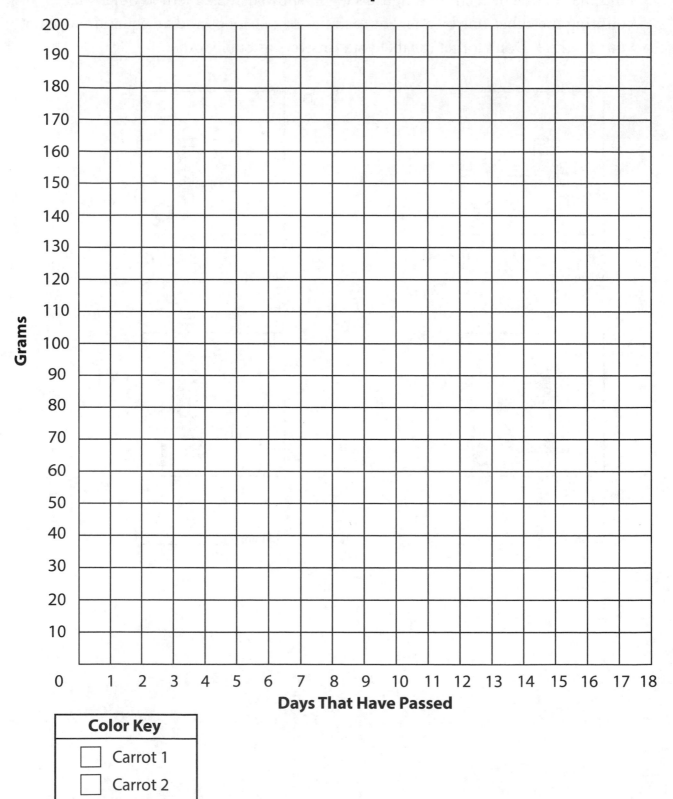

Another Carrot Experiment page 1 of 2

Mrs. Ozuna's class left a carrot sitting out for 12 days. The students measured its mass nearly every day and made a line graph to show what happened. Use the graph to answer the questions.

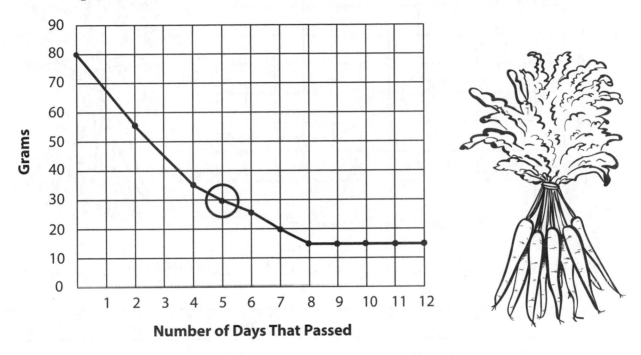

1 What was the carrot's mass when the experiment started (Day 0)?

2 How much mass did the carrot lose in the first 2 days?

3 How many days did it take until the carrot stopped losing any mass at all?

4 On which day was the mass of the carrot 35 grams?

5 How much more mass did the carrot lose during the first four days (Days 0–4) than during the four days after that (Days 4–8)?

6 What is the meaning of the circled point on the graph? Use carrots, ounces, and days in your answer.

Another Carrot Experiment page 2 of 2

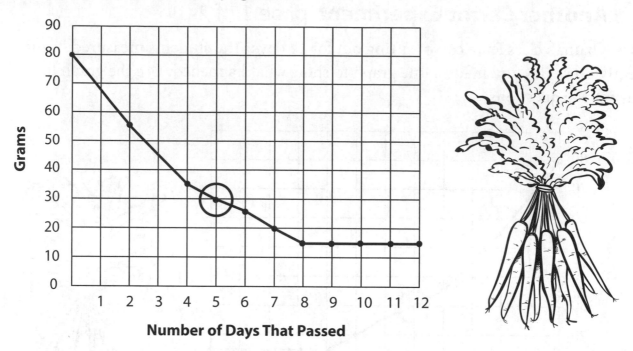

7 The class left a second carrot sitting out for 12 days. Here's the data they collected. Enter it on the graph above.

Day	Mass	Day	Mass	Day	Mass
Starting Weight	90 grams	Day 6	52 grams	Day 10	40 grams
Day 2	75 grams	Day 7	50 grams	Day 11	40 grams
Day 4	60 grams	Day 8	45 grams	Day 12	40 grams
Day 5	53 grams	Day 9	40 grams		

8 Write at least four sentences about how this carrot experiment was similar to and different from your own class's carrot experiment.

⊞ Grouping Symbols

1 Use the information from the teacher master on display to help answer questions a and b below.

a List at least three of the different answers you and your classmates found for $8 + 3 \times 3 - 1$.

b For each different answer, write $8 + 3 \times 3 - 1$ with parentheses to show how you got that answer.

2 Mr. Delaney gave his fifth graders an equation to solve. The kids got four different answers, and Mr. Delaney said they were all correct.

a Place parentheses where they need to be in each equation to make it true.

b Do the operations in the order you've shown to prove that your solutions work.

$10 \times 5 + 2 \div 2 = 26$	$10 \times 5 + 2 \div 2 = 51$
$10 \times 5 + 2 \div 2 = 35$	$10 \times 5 + 2 \div 2 = 60$

NAME _____ | DATE _____

⊞⊟ Group It! Instructions & Record Sheet
⊡⊠

1 Decide who will be the Red Team and who will be the Blue, and record your names.

2 On your turn, spin the spinner to find out if you have to use grouping symbols to get the answer, or to create the answer.

3 After you spin, circle one of the equations in the correct column with your team's color. Then use parentheses to find the answer given or make the highest answer possible.

Do the operations in the order you've shown to prove that your solutions work.

4 Take turns until each team has had 3 turns. Then add up your answers to get your total score. The team with the higher score wins the game.

If you spin and all the equations in the designated column have been used, you have to choose one of the equations in the other column.

Red Team: _____ Blue Team:_____

Get the Answer	Create an Answer
$24 + 8 \div 4 - 6 + 14 = 6$	$12 \div 4 + 2 \times 5 = $ _____
$16 \times \frac{1}{4} + 5 \times 7 = 63$	$25 \times \frac{2}{5} + \frac{3}{5} \times 15 - 2 = $ _____
$2 + 5 \times 6 \times \frac{1}{3} + 6 = 56$	$3 \times 4 + 10 \div 2 = $ _____
$7 + 8 - 6 \times 9 = 81$	$14 - 6 \div 2 \times 10 = $ _____

Red Team Total Score:_____ Blue Team Total Score: _____

16

NAME _____ | **DATE** _____

⊞ **Partner Group It!**

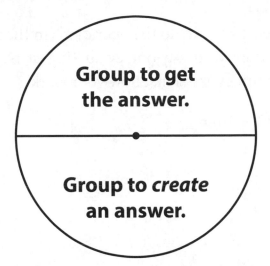

Group to get
the answer.

Group to *create*
an answer.

Red Team: _____   Blue Team: _____

Get the Answer	Create an Answer
$48 \div 4 - 3 + 1 \times 5 = 40$	$7 \times 6 - 9 + \frac{1}{3} \times 15 \div 2 = $ _____
$13 - 6 \div 2 + 1 = 11$	$36 \div 4 + 2 \times 7 = $ _____
$15 \div 3 + 2 \times 5 - \frac{1}{2} = 14\frac{1}{2}$	$\frac{1}{2} \times 60 + 15 \div 3 = $ _____
$8 \times 8 - 6 \times 6 = 96$	$6 \times 3 + 7 - 1 \times 4 = $ _____
$\frac{1}{3} \times 60 + 15 \div 3 = 25$	$20 \times \frac{1}{4} + \frac{3}{4} + 6 = $ _____

Red Team Total Score: _____   Blue Team Total Score: _____

NAME _____ | DATE _____

⊞ Using Parentheses to Make Groups

1 Solve each equation. Remember to do the operations in the innermost set of parentheses first, then work your way out, evaluating each group of parentheses until you have evaluated the full expression. Show your work.

a $463 - (180 \div (3 \times (3 + 3))) =$ _____

b $((249 - 222) \div 3) \times 12 =$ _____

c $((36 + 14) \times (182 - 164)) \div 10 =$ _____

2 Insert parentheses to create the *largest* answer possible, and record your answer. Do the operations in the order you've shown to prove that your solutions work.

a $16 \times 2 + 7 \times 5 =$ _____

b $4 + 2 \times 5 - 12 \div 6 =$ _____

c $65 + 18 \div 2 + \frac{1}{2} \times 10 =$ _____

3 Insert parentheses to make each equation true. Do the operations in the order you've shown to prove that your solutions work.

a $3 \times 9 + 18 + 36 \div 9 = 33$ **b** $140 \div 2 + 12 - 4 \times 2 = 2$

18

NAME | **DATE**

 So Many Possibilities page 1 of 2

Use the blank space to solve each problem. Show all your work including numbers, words, or labeled sketches. Write a complete sentence below your work to show the answer.

1 Mr. Mugwump is planning a party and he's going to serve ice-cream sundaes to his friends. He has 3 different flavors of ice cream: vanilla, chocolate, and strawberry. He has three different toppings: jelly beans, nuts, and berries. If you get to choose 1 flavor of ice cream and 1 topping for a sundae, how many different sundaes can be made? List all the possibilities. (One of them is vanilla and jelly beans. What are the rest?)

NAME | **DATE**

So Many Possibilities page 2 of 2

2 Maggie is buying party favors for her birthday party. She has $5.00 to spend. She can buy pencils for $.50 each, rubber balls for $1.00 each, and yo-yos for $1.50 each. How many different combinations of these party favors can she buy with her $5.00? Show your work. Use a separate sheet of paper if necessary.

pencil   rubber ball   yo-yo

3 Dana went to the Dollar Store with a few coins in her pocket, including pennies, nickels, dimes, and quarters. She knew that she could pay for any item from 1¢ up to $1.00 without getting any change back. If something cost 7¢ or 18¢ or 23¢ or 89¢ or any other price up through exactly $1.00, she could use her coins to pay for it exactly. How many coins did Dana have in her pocket and what were they? (Find the fewest number of coins possible.)

💡 **Pattern Puzzles** page 1 of 2

Use the blank space to solve each problem. Show all your work including numbers, words, or labeled sketches. Write a complete sentence below your work to show the answer.

1 How many different ways are there to make 20¢ with pennies, nickels, and dimes?

2 What is the smallest number (greater than 1) that is both triangular and square?

1, 3, 6, and 10 are called triangular numbers because they can be arranged like this:	1, 4, 9, and 16 are called square numbers because they can be arranged like this:

Pattern Puzzles page 2 of 2

3 Mr. Mugwump invented an unusual clock. When you take it out of the box and press the start button, it chimes once after the first minute has passed. It chimes again when 2 minutes have passed. It chimes again when a total of 4 minutes have passed, then again after 8 minutes, then again after 16 minutes, and so on. How many times will this clock have chimed when 30 days have passed?

NAME _____ | DATE _____

 Patty's Plant Shop page 1 of 2

Patty has a small shop where she sells many different kinds of plants and flowers. Sometimes her customers get confused about where to find certain varieties, so Patty created the map showing the floor plan of her shop, below, to help them.

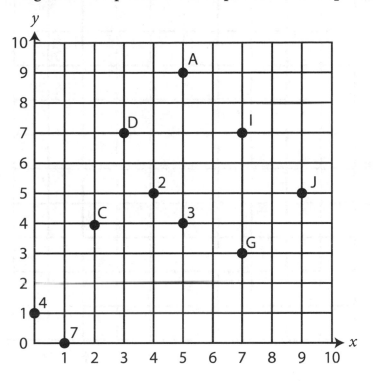

1 Identify and record the coordinates for the flowers.

Calla lily (C) _____

Iris (I) _____

Daisy (D) _____

Geranium (G) _____

2 Patty got four new kinds of flowers to sell. She has four open areas in the shop (labeled 1, 2, 3, and 4 on her map). Use the coordinates given to tell where each flower is located.

a Begonias (5, 4) are located in area _____.

b Roses (1, 0) are located in area _____.

c Petunias (4, 5) are located in area _____.

d Snapdragons (0, 1) are located in area _____.

(continued on next page)

Patty's Plant Shop page 2 of 2

3 Patty bought a new table to use for displays. Use the points given to sketch the table in its correct location. (4,7), (8,7), (8,9), (4,9)

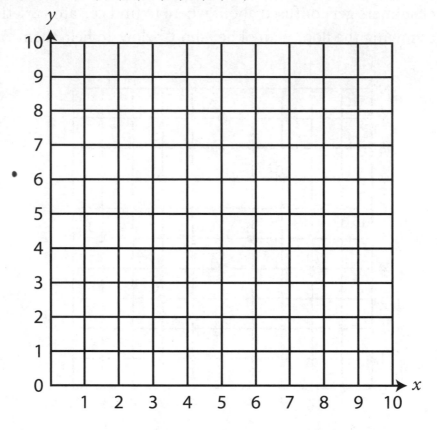

4 If each linear unit on the grid above represents 1 yard, what are the dimensions of Patty's table? In other words, how wide and how long is Patty's table?

a What is the area of Patty's table, in square yards?

NAME _____ **|DATE** _____

 Meters, Meters & More Meters

1 Fill in the table.

centimeters	100	200	400		1,000	1,500			
meters	1			7			20	25	100

2 Fill in the table.

decameters	1			3	3.1	10	25		
meters	10	20	25					560	1,000

3 Fill in the table.

kilometers	0.001				0.4	1	2.1	3			
meters	1	25	50	100					4,000	4,500	5,000

4 Round 2,365.78

a To the nearest tenth _____

b To the nearest one _____

c To the nearest ten _____

d To the nearest hundred _____

e To the nearest thousand _____

5 Cameron said, "Since there are 1,000 meters in a kilometer, meters must be bigger than kilometers." Respond to Cameron.

NAME _____ | **DATE** _____

 Expression Bingo Board A

11	**54**	**28**	**80**
40	**18**	**56**	**27**
8	**2**	**48**	**26**
6	**60**	**42**	**33**

_____

_____

_____

_____

_____

_____

_____

_____

_____

Expression Bingo Board B

48	**2**	**54**	**26**
80	**27**	**42**	**40**
6	**60**	**11**	**28**
56	**18**	**8**	**33**

NAME _____ | DATE _____

⊞ Simplifying Expressions

1 Solve each expression.

a $((40 \times 2) - 10) \div 5 =$ _____

b _____ $= ((6 \times 3) - 3) \times (4 \times 5)$

c _____ $= (9 \times 3) + ((4 \times 16) + 8))$

2 Add parentheses to make each equation true.

a $5 + 3 \times 2 \div 4 = 4$

b $17 = 4 \times 5 - 1 \times 4 + 1$

c $3 \times 3 \times 7 + 4 - 1 = 90$

3 Sarah and Haley were selling items to raise money for their volleyball team. Their goal was to raise $360. They sold headbands for $6 each, colored socks for $4 a pair, and team T-shirts for $15 each.

a Sarah sold 4 headbands and 3 T-shirts during the first week. Write an expression to show her sales.

b Simplify the expression in part a to find Sarah's total sales.

c Haley sold 2 T-shirts, 2 headbands, and 3 pairs of socks during the first week. Write an expression to show her sales.

d Simplify the expression in part c to find Haley's total sales.

4 After three weeks, the girls together had sold 12 headbands, 11 T-shirts, and 6 pairs of socks.

a Write an expression to show how much more the girls need to sell to reach their goal.

b Simplify the expression in part a.

Figuring with Fractions page 1 of 2

1 Use the blank space to solve each problem. Show all your work including numbers, words, or labeled sketches.

a Henry has a bag of marbles. Six of them are striped. The other half of the marbles are not striped. How many marbles does Harold have in his bag?

b Julissa has a bag with 6 white marbles and some more black marbles. One-third of the marbles are white. How many marbles does she have in all?

c Mr. Smith has a big bag of marbles. Six of the marbles are green. There are also 6 marbles in each of these colors: blue, red, yellow, and white. How many marbles are in Mr. Smith's bag in all?

2 You can use these arrays of 36 to help you solve the problems below.

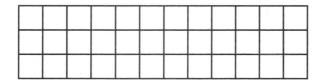

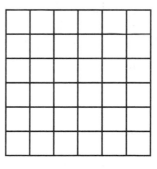

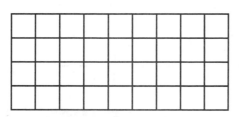

a What is $\frac{1}{2}$ of 36?

b What is $\frac{1}{4}$ of 36?

c What is $\frac{3}{4}$ of 36?

d What is $\frac{1}{3}$ of 36?

e What is $\frac{2}{3}$ of 36?

f What is $\frac{1}{6}$ of 36?

g What is $\frac{5}{6}$ of 36?

(continued on next page)

Figuring with Fractions page 2 of 2

3 A kindergarten class has a box of blocks. Some blocks are red, some are yellow, and some are blue. Given the information below, determine how many blocks are in the box, and explain your thinking.

- $\frac{1}{2}$ of the blocks are red
- $\frac{1}{4}$ of the blocks are yellow
- 24 of the blocks are blue

4 If the area of the gray square in the design shown below is 16 square units, what is the area of each of the other squares in the design, including the large square that contains all the smaller squares?

Categorizing & Drawing Quadrilaterals page 1 of 2

1 Write the name of each shape under it. Choose from this list of words. You can use more than one word for each shape.

| parallelogram | kite | rhombus | quadrilateral | trapezoid | square | rectangle |

2 Draw a line from the shape to the name of the shape. For some shapes, you will need to draw lines to more than one word.

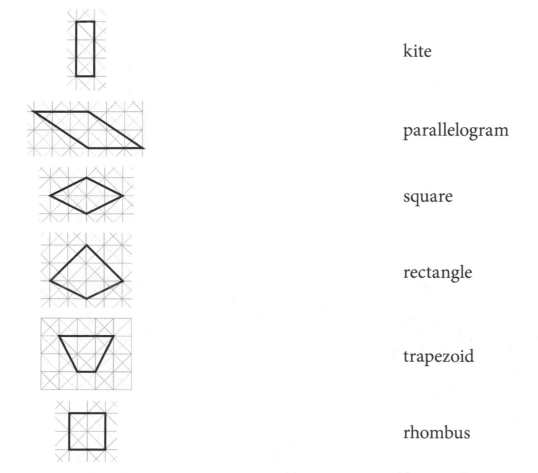

kite

parallelogram

square

rectangle

trapezoid

rhombus

Categorizing & Drawing Quadrilaterals page 1 of 2

3 Draw each shape named below. One side is provided for you each time.

a kite

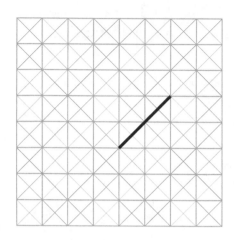

b square

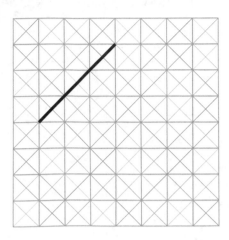

c parallelogram

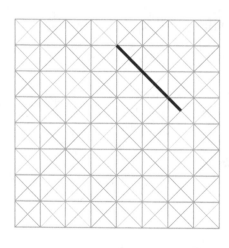

d trapezoid

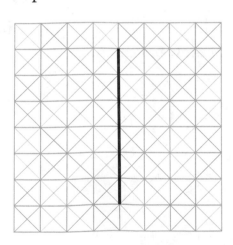

e CHALLENGE square

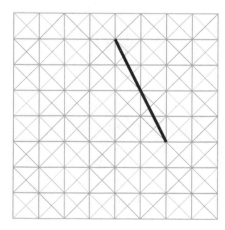

Line Plot Problems

Use the two line plots you created as a class to answer these questions.

1 Look at the class heights line plot.

a What is the height of the tallest person in our class in inches?

b What is the height of the shortest person in our class in inches?

c How many inches taller is the tallest person in our class than the shortest person in our class?

2 Look at the class foot length line plot.

a What is the longest foot length in our class?

b What is the shortest foot length in our class?

c How many inches longer is the longest foot than the shortest foot?

3 How would you describe the heights of the students in our class to someone who cannot see us?

4 How would you describe the foot lengths of students in our class to someone who cannot see us?

Creating Data Displays

When Greg and his friends were helping in the school garden, they found many earthworms. They collected 10 earthworms, measured them to the nearest eighth of an inch, and recorded those measurements here.

Worm 1	$2\frac{1}{8}$ inches	**Worm 5**	$2\frac{6}{8}$ inches	**Worm 9**	$2\frac{5}{8}$ inches
Worm 2	$2\frac{6}{8}$ inches	**Worm 6**	$3\frac{4}{8}$ inches	**Worm 10**	3 inches
Worm 3	$4\frac{3}{8}$ inches	**Worm 7**	$5\frac{1}{8}$ inches		
Worm 4	$3\frac{5}{8}$ inches	**Worm 8**	$4\frac{2}{8}$ inches		

1 Create a line plot with this data.

○ Label the line so that all of the measurements can be shown on it.

○ Make an X to show each measurement on the line plot.

○ Write a title for the line plot here: _____

_____

_____

_____

_____

2 How long was the longest worm?

3 How long was the shortest worm?

4 How much longer was the longest worm than the shortest worm?

5 How would you describe the length of the typical worm that Greg found in this garden?

Make an Informed Start

1 The Sweet Tooth Bakery sells cupcakes for $1.50 each. They also sell boxes of 10 cupcakes for $15 per box. The bakery has the following price lists to help customers. Complete each price list. Then use the price lists to solve the following problems.

Individual Cupcakes	
Number of Cupcakes	**Total Price**
1	$1.50
2	
4	
10	
5	
9	
20	

Boxes of Cupcakes *10 cupcakes per box*	
Number of Boxes	**Total Price**
1	$15
2	
4	
10	
5	
9	
20	

a How much would it cost to buy 42 individual cupcakes?

b Write an equation to show how you could determine the total price for 42 cupcakes.

c How much would it cost to buy 42 boxes of cupcakes?

d How many cupcakes are in 42 boxes?

e Write an equation to show how you could determine the total price for 42 boxes of cupcakes.

2 **CHALLENGE** The Sugar & Spice Bakery sells cupcakes for $1.35 each and boxes of 10 cupcakes for $13.50.

a How much would it cost to buy 13 cupcakes at Sugar & Spice?

b How much would it cost to buy 13 boxes of cupcakes at Sugar & Spice?

3 **CHALLENGE** To make a carrot cake, the baker at Sugar & Spice uses $\frac{1}{3}$ pound of walnuts. If she plans to make 38 carrot cakes this week, how many pounds of walnuts will she use?

Graphing Coordinates

1 Complete this table for the four markers you will be graphing.

Marker	Term (x)	Total Squares (y)	Coordinates (x,y)	Equation
	0			
	1			
	2			
	3			

2 Write an equation that shows how the x and y values in the table above are related.

3 Graph the coordinates on this coordinate grid.

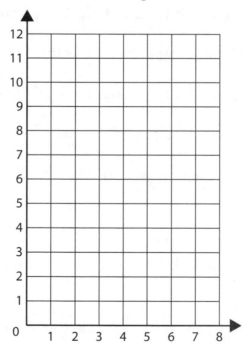

4 Use your graph and the equation you wrote to answer these questions.

a How many squares would be in term 4 of the sequence?

b How many squares would be in term 10 of the sequence?

c How many squares would be in term 50 of the sequence?

Graphing Two Patterns

Write a statement that describes the rule for each equation in words. Then complete the table of coordinates for each equation. Then graph the coordinates and connect the points to show the line.

1 $x + 2 = y$

a Statement:

b Complete the table of coordinates.

Term (x)	Total (y)	Coordinates (x,y)
0		
1		
2		
3		

c Graph the coordinates and connect them to show the line.

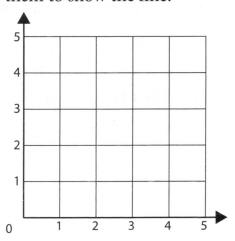

2 $2x + 2 = y$

a Statement:

b Complete the table of coordinates.

Term (x)	Total (y)	Coordinates (x,y)
0		
1		
2		
3		

c Graph the coordinates and connect them to show the line.

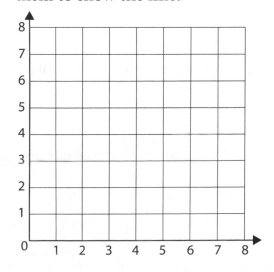

37

First Week Earnings

1 How much time has Susan earned so far?

   a   List the fractional amounts of time (for electronics use) that Susan has earned so far.

   b   How much time has Susan earned?

   c   What other representations can be recorded to represent the same amount?

2 How much money has Susan earned so far?

   a   List the fractional amounts of money (allowance) that Susan has earned so far.

   b   How much money has Susan earned?

   c   What other representations can be recorded to represent the same amount?

NAME _____ **| DATE** _____

 ## Susan's Goals

1 Susan keeps track of the money and time she earns in a journal. Fill in the missing information for a portion of Susan's journal.

Earnings				
Days	**Time Earned**	**Total Hours Earned**	**Money Earned**	**Total Money Earned**
1 & 2	$3 \times \frac{1}{10}$ of an hour		$4 \times \frac{1}{5}$ dollars	
3 & 4	$2 \times \frac{1}{6}$ of an hour		$2 \times \frac{1}{4}$ dollars	
5 & 6	$6 \times \frac{1}{6}$ of an hour		$6 \times \frac{1}{2}$ dollars	

2 After the first 6 days, Susan decides to spend her earnings.

a If she spends $\frac{1}{3}$ of an hour on electronics time, how much time does she have left? Write your answer in fraction form.

b If she spends $\frac{3}{4}$ of a dollar, how much money does she have left? Write your answer in fractions and decimals.

3 Susan set a goal of earning $20 for the month. When she looks at her journal, she sees that she earned 14 one-half dollars, 22 one-fourth dollars, and 11 one-fifth dollars. Has Susan reached her goal? If so, is she over the goal and by how much? If not, how far from her goal is she?

4 Write a question relating to Susan earning or spending time or money.

39

NAME _____ | **DATE** _____

⊞ Color Ten, Version 1

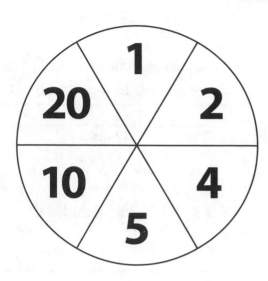

- Each player gets 5 spins.
- You can choose to use fourths, fifths, or tenths. You can't mix fractions in a single spin.
- You must use all 5 turns.
- Use a different color for each turn.
- The player that gets closest (either over or under) to coloring in 10 grids wins.

Fractions spun _____

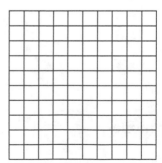 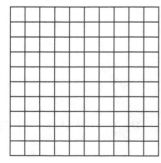 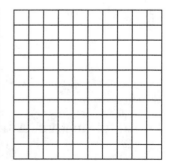 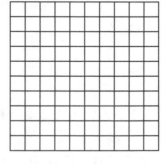

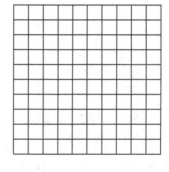 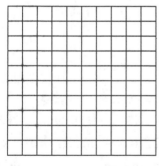 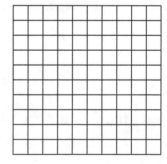 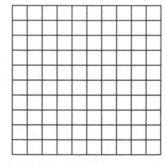

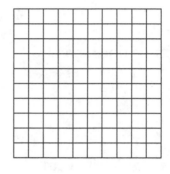 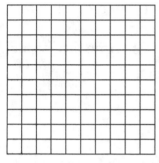 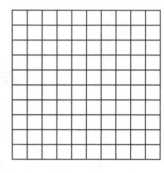 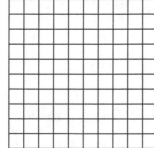

40

NAME _____ | DATE _____

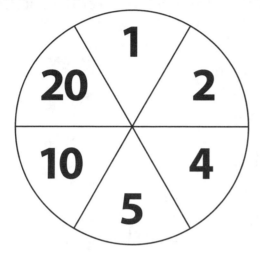 Color Ten, Version 2

- For each turn, spin both spinners one time. Spinner 1 indicates the numerator. You can choose to use fourths, fifths, or tenths as the denominator.

- Spinner 2 indicates how many of the fractions you created that you must shade in.

- You must use all 5 turns and use a different color for each turn.

- The player that gets closest (either over or under) to coloring in 10 grids wins.

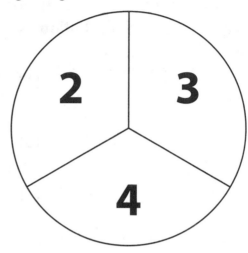

Fractions spun _____

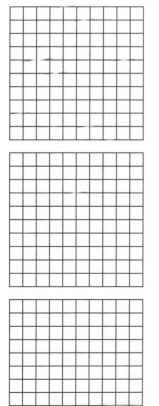 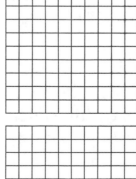 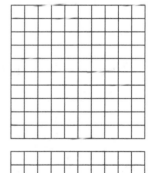

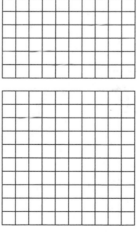 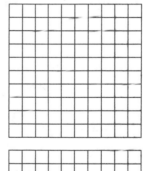 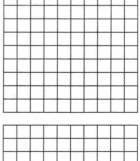

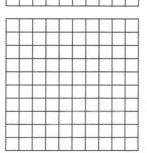 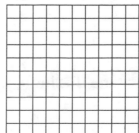

💡 Buildings in Blocktown page 1 of 2

Luke's favorite hobby is to create buildings for his fictional community, Blocktown. Sometimes Luke imagines what interesting buildings would look like, and sometimes he copies pictures or actual buildings he sees. All the buildings he makes consist of rectangular prisms put together. To make his buildings, Luke uses small blocks that measure 1 by 1 by 1 unit, and each block costs $0.05 at the store. Answer the questions below to help Luke with his buildings.

1 Luke wants to make a building like the one shown.

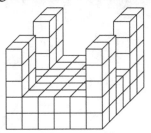

    a What is the volume of the building (how many cubes will he need)?

    b Find the cost to create this building.

2 Luke wants to make another building like the one shown.

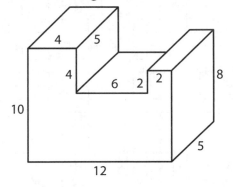

    a What is the volume of the building?

    b Find the cost to create this building.

(continued on next page)

Buildings in Blocktown page 2 of 2

3 Luke wants to make a 1-layer building like the one shown, where the building has only 1 floor and 4 openings in the middle for landscaping.

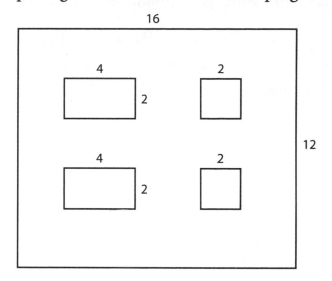

a What is the volume of the actual building, not including the landscape areas?

b Find the cost to create this building.

4 Luke wants to make a building that has a volume of 24 cubics units for its base. He wondered what the volume would be for multiple layers. He also wondered how many layers he could make with a given volume. Fill in the ratio table below to help Luke with his questions.

Volume	24	48		240			576
Height	1	2	5		15	25	

5 **CHALLENGE** How much will it cost Luke to make a 20-layer building, if the base volume is 24 cubic units?

💡 Better Buildings

1 Luke's mom surprised him with an additional 80 blocks to use in Blocktown.

    a If he makes a construction consisting of only rectangular prisms stuck together, and uses all 80, how could the building be made? Sketch the building and label the dimensions.

    b Show how you know the volume of the building is 80 cubic units. Record an equation.

2 Luke saved $5.45 from allowance.

    a What is the maximum number of blocks could he buy?

    b Assume Luke used all of his savings to buy new blocks. Draw a building he could add to Blocktown, using only the blocks from his recent purchase.

Fraction Multiplication Grid Area Key

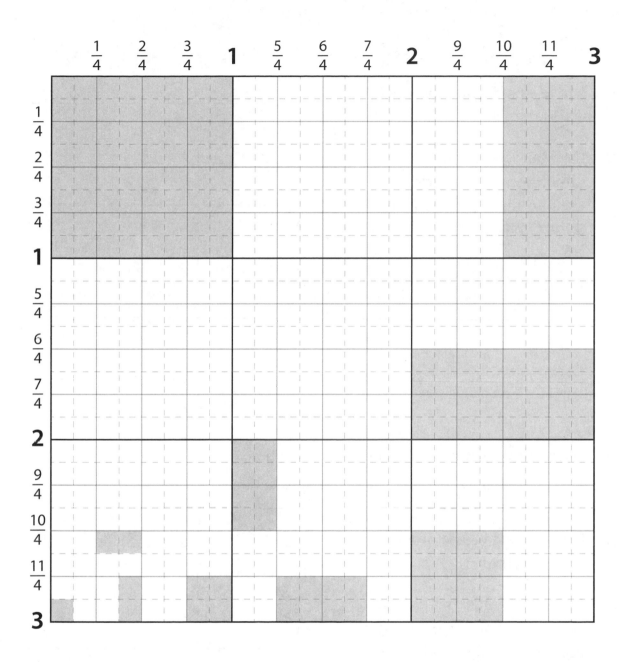

45

NAME _____ | **DATE** _____

Multiplying with Fractions page 1 of 2

1 Look carefully at the pairs of numbers shown here.

$$\frac{3}{4} \times \frac{1}{2} \qquad \frac{3}{4} \times 1\frac{7}{8} \qquad \frac{1}{4} \times \frac{3}{8} \qquad 1\frac{1}{2} \times \frac{1}{2} \qquad 2 \times \frac{1}{4} \qquad 2\frac{1}{4} \times \frac{3}{4}$$

a Circle a pair whose product is less than 1.

b Draw a rectangle with these dimensions on the grid and use it to find the product of these two numbers.

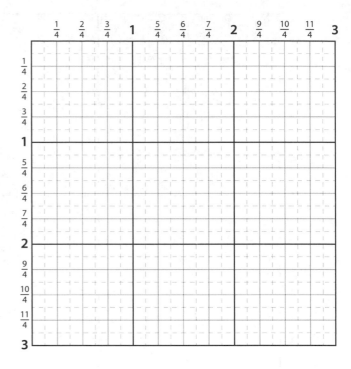

2 Look carefully at the pairs of numbers shown here.

$$\frac{3}{4} \times \frac{1}{4} \qquad \frac{1}{2} \times 2\frac{3}{4} \qquad 1\frac{1}{4} \times 1\frac{3}{8} \qquad 1\frac{1}{4} \times \frac{1}{2} \qquad \frac{3}{4} \times \frac{1}{2} \qquad 2 \times \frac{3}{4}$$

a Circle a pair whose product is greater than 1.

b Draw a rectangle with these dimensions on the grid and use it to find the product of these two numbers.

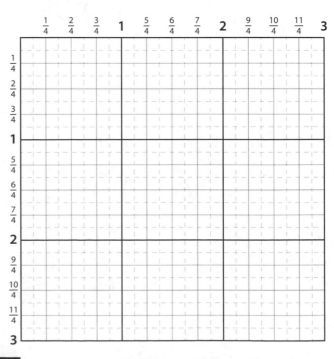

46

NAME _____ | DATE _____

Multiplying with Fractions page 2 of 2

3 Draw and label two different rectangles with an area of $\frac{3}{4}$ square unit.

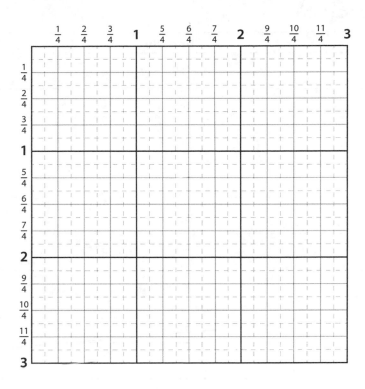

4 Draw and label two different rectangles with an area of $1\frac{1}{2}$ square units.

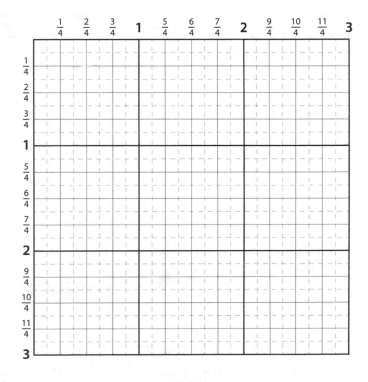

NAME _____ | **DATE** _____

 # Liters, Deciliters & Milliliters

Each row in this table shows a single liquid volume expressed in liters, deciliters, and milliliters. Complete the table.

Liters (l)	Deciliters (dl)	Milliliters (ml)
1	10	1000
	1	
		1
		500
	50	
		370
		836
	82	
2.5		

Use the table below to record the equivalencies for the Two Liters or Spill Spinner.

Liters (l)	Deciliters (dl)	Milliliters (ml)
	0.25	
0.20		
	0.50	
0.25		
	0.20	
0.10		

Measuring Liquid Volume

In the United States, milk, juice, and other liquids are measured in ounces, cups, pints, quarts, and gallons. Use the information shown to complete each ratio table.

1

cups	1	2	3		
ounces					

2

quarts	1	2	3		
ounces					

3

gallons	1	2	3		
ounces					

 1 ounce (oz.)

 1 cup (c.) = 8 ounces

 1 pint (pt.) = 2 cups

 1 quart (qt.) = 4 cups

 1 gallon (gal.) = 4 quarts

4 Answer the following questions by using and completing the appropriate ratio table. How many ounces are in:

a $\frac{1}{2}$ cup?

b 10 cups?

c $\frac{1}{2}$ quart?

d 6 quarts?

e $\frac{1}{2}$ gallon?

In other countries around the world, liquid volume is measured in milliliters and liters. Use the information shown to complete the ratio table.

5

liters	1	2	3		
milliliters					

 1 liter (l) = 1,000 milliliters (ml)

6 How many milliliters are in:

a $\frac{1}{2}$ of a liter?

b $\frac{1}{4}$ of a liter?

🔆 Measuring Problems

1 Roxanne set a goal of drinking 2.5 liters of water each day. By 10:00 a.m., she drank $\frac{3}{4}$ liter, and at lunch she had another 600 ml. In the afternoon, she purchased a bottle of water that contained 1.1 liters.

    a If Roxanne finishes the bottle, will she have reached her goal for the day?

    b How far over or under her goal is she?

2 Some of Roxanne's bottles are measured in liters and some are measured in milliliters. Convert the following:

    a 1,500 milliliters = _____ liters   **b** _____ milliliters = 1.25 liters

    c 0.3 liters = _____ milliliters   **d** 10 milliliters = _____ liters

    e 280 milliliters = _____ liters

    f Explain how Roxanne can use patterns to multiply or divide by powers of 10.

3 Jackson and his little brother together drank a quart of milk on Tuesday and another pint of milk on Wednesday morning.

    a How many cups of milk did they drink?

    b If Jackson drank $\frac{2}{3}$ of the milk on those two days, how many ounces did each boy have?

4 Briana likes to make up new recipes. Yesterday, she combined $\frac{1}{4}$ cup of pear juice, $\frac{1}{4}$ cup of grape juice, $\frac{1}{8}$ cup of lime juice, 1 cup of cranberry juice, and $1\frac{1}{2}$ cups of lemon-lime soda to make her own fruit punch. How many ounces of fruit punch did Briana have?

Multiplying Decimal Numbers page 1 of 2

1 428 × 56

    a Estimate a reasonable solution to the problem and write it here: _____

    b Find the exact product.

    c Find the exact product for the following combinations.

42.8 × 56	428 × 5.6	42.8 × 5.6

2 603 × 87

    a Estimate a reasonable solution to the problem and write it here: _____

    b Find the exact product.

    c Find the exact product for the following combinations.

60.3 × 8.7	6.03 × 8.7	6.03 × 0.87

Multiplying Decimal Numbers page 2 of 2

3 218 × 745

    a Estimate a reasonable solution to the problem and write it here: _____

    b Find the exact product.

    c Write an expression showing two numbers that would have a product that is one-tenth the product of 218 × 745.

    d Write an expression showing two numbers that would have a product that is one-hundredth the product of 218 × 745.

4 Circle all the combinations with a value that is one-hundredth of 837 × 309.

0.837 × 309	83.7 × 30.9	8.37 × 309
837 × 3.09	8.37 × 3.09	837 × 0.309

Pencil Length Over Time

Measure the length of your pencil to the nearest eighth of an inch. Record the length of your pencil at the following times.

before sharpening	after sharpening 1 time
after 1 week of use	after 2 weeks of use
after 3 weeks of use	after 4 weeks of use

Line Plot Problems 1

Use the line plot you just created as a class to answer the following questions.

1   How long was the longest pencil?

2   How long was the shortest pencil?

3   How much longer is the longest pencil than the shortest pencil?

4   Find a set of pencils shown on the line plot that all have the same length.

   a   How long is each pencil?

   b   How many pencils have that same length?

   c   If you lined them all up, how long would they be together?

5   How long was your pencil?

6   On the line plot, find a pencil that is longer than yours and calculate exactly how much longer it is than yours. If yours is longest, calculate how much longer it is than the next longest pencil.

7   On the line plot, find a pencil that is shorter than yours and calculate exactly how much shorter it is than yours. If yours is shortest, calculate how much shorter it is than the next shortest pencil.

Line Plot Problems 2

Use the line plot you just created as a class to answer the following questions.

1 How long was the longest pencil? _____

2 How long was the shortest pencil? _____

3 How much longer is the longer pencil than the shorter pencil?

4 Find a set of pencils shown on the line plot that all have the same length.

   a How long is each pencil? _____

   b How many pencils have that same length? _____

   c If you lined them all up, how long would they be together?

5 How long was your pencil? _____

6 On the line plot, find a pencil that is longer than yours and calculate exactly how much longer it is than yours. If yours is longest, calculate how much longer it is than the next longest pencil.

7 On the line plot, find a pencil that is shorter than yours and calculate exactly how much shorter it is than yours. If yours is shortest, calculate how much shorter it is than the next shortest pencil.

8 How is this line plot similar to the line plot from last week?

9 How is this line plot different from the line plot from last week?

Line Plots & Story Problems page 1 of 2

Some fifth graders measured the length of each carrot in a bag of mini carrots from the cafeteria. These are their measurements.

$3\frac{1}{4}$ $2\frac{5}{8}$ $2\frac{1}{2}$ $1\frac{7}{8}$ 2 2 $1\frac{7}{8}$ $2\frac{5}{8}$ 2 $2\frac{3}{4}$ 2 $2\frac{3}{8}$ $3\frac{1}{4}$ $2\frac{1}{2}$

1   Create a line plot to show this data. Then answer the questions that follow.

_____
Title

_____

2   What is the length of the shortest carrot? _____

3   What is the length of the longest carrot? _____

4   What is the difference in length between the longest and shortest carrots?

5   If they placed all the carrots that measured $2\frac{5}{8}$ inches end to end, how long would the line of carrots be?

Line Plots & Story Problems page 2 of 2

6 If you had a regular carrot that was $6\frac{5}{8}$ inches long, and you took a bite out of it that was $2\frac{1}{4}$ inch long, how long would the carrot be?

7 Jason had a regular carrot. He took a bite out of it that was $1\frac{1}{4}$ inches long. After he took the bite, the carrot was $5\frac{1}{8}$ inches long. How long was the carrot before he took the bite?

8 **CHALLENGE** The fifth graders placed 4 carrots from a different bag that all had the same length end to end. Altogether, they had a length of $9\frac{1}{2}$ inches. How long was each carrot?

57

Quotient Bingo Board 1

4.9	0.125	510	2.2	99
22	990	0.15	7.5	12.5
0.75	1.5	FREE	15	5.1
3.5	220	9.9	49	0.075
51	0.35	350	1.25	490

58

NAME _____ | DATE _____

Quotient Bingo Board 2

420	15	17.5	42	0.175
6.25	0.125	45	0.25	150
0.075	2.5	FREE	0.75	1.25
4.2	1.75	7.5	0.625	25
62.5	0.45	1.5	12.5	4.5

NAME _____ | DATE _____

Quotient Bingo Board 3

32	0.175	98	0.75	3.2
1.25	0.8	15	12.5	0.08
1.75	75	FREE	7.5	980
150	0.25	8	25	0.125
2.5	9.8	320	17.5	1.5

1 $256 \div 8$

2 $5 \div 4$

3 $195 \div 13$

4 $28 \div 16$

5 $15 \div 2$

6 $1,078 \div 11$

7 $8 \div 10$

8 $10 \div 4$

NAME _____ | DATE _____

⊞ Quotient Bingo Board 4

21	42	0.16	210	0.24
0.8	1.6	0.08	36	7.5
75	3.6	FREE	7.2	0.42
24	4.2	2.1	80	2.4
72	16	0.36	0.72	750

1 $4 \div 5$

2 $18 \div 5$

3 $21 \div 5$

4 $8 \div 5$

5 $12 \div 5$

6 $36 \div 5$

7 $315 \div 15$

8 $6{,}750 \div 90$

Problem Set 1

1 Andre ran a total of 657 miles during the past 36 days. His goal is to run 1,000 miles in 60 days.

    a The problem I am solving about this situation is:

    b Use this space to solve the problem and record your thinking with numbers, words, equations or models.

    c Solution:

2 In a school election, Yolanda got 160 more votes than Alex, and Alex got twice as many votes as Jennifer. A total of 440 votes were cast.

    a The problem I am solving about this situation is:

    b Use this space to solve the problem and record your thinking with numbers, words, equations or models.

    c Solution:

💡 Problem Set 2

1 Dustin's favorite ice cream is on sale for $3.84 a gallon. He has $20.

  a The problem I am solving about this situation is:

  b Use this space to solve the problem and record your thinking with numbers, words, equations or models.

  c Solution:

2 For the neighborhood barbecue tomorrow, Corey bought 3.4 pounds of hamburger that cost $1.67 a pound. Erika spent $5.90 on 3.6 pounds of hamburger.

  a The problem I am solving about this situation is:

  b Use this space to solve the problem and record your thinking with numbers, words, equations or models.

  c Solution:

NAME _____ | **DATE** _____

 ## Volume & Surface Area Patterns

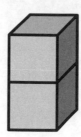 The *volume* of a solid figure is the number of cubes of a given size it takes to build that figure. Volume is measured in cubic units, or cubes.

This figure took 2 centimeter cubes to build, so its volume is 2 cubic centimeters (2 cm³).

1 Here are the figures on markers 6–10 this month. Find the volume of each. Remember to label your measurements with the correct units.

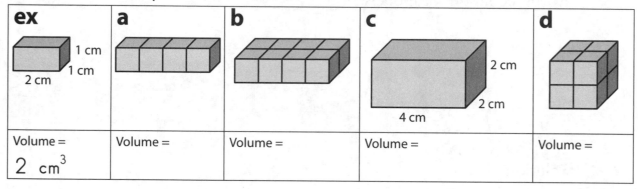

ex	a	b	c	d
1 cm, 1 cm, 2 cm			2 cm, 2 cm, 4 cm	
Volume = 2 cm³	Volume =	Volume =	Volume =	Volume =

2 Use numbers to show to show how you found the volume of figure c above.

3 List at least 3 different patterns you see among the volumes of the five figures above.

More About Volume page 1 of 2

1 Here are the figures on the last five markers this month. Find the volume of each one. Remember to label your measurements with the correct units. (The first figure has been done for you.)

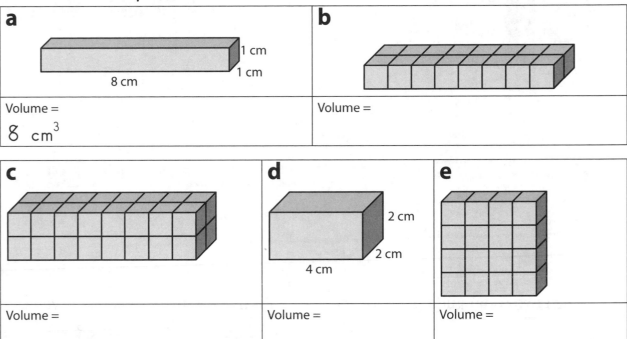

a

8 cm
1 cm
1 cm

Volume =

8 cm³

b

Volume =

c

Volume =

d

4 cm
2 cm
2 cm

Volume =

e

Volume =

2 Use numbers to show how you found the volume of figure d above.

(continued on next page)

More About Volume page 2 of 2

3 Find the volume of this rectangular prism. Show your work.

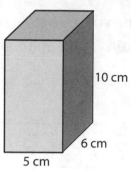

10 cm

6 cm

5 cm

4 Which two rectangular prisms below show the same volume? Explain how you can tell.

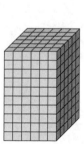 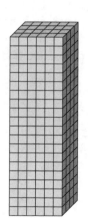 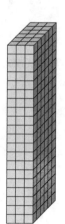 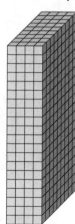

NAME _____ | **DATE** _____

 # Solving Fraction Problems

1 Imagine we kept on collecting $\frac{3}{4}$ of a dollar and an hour each day. After how many days would we have a whole number of dollars and hours? (Circle all that apply.)

36   42   50   64

2 Find each sum or difference. Show your work using numbers or pictures. Consider using a number line.

$3\frac{1}{4} + \frac{1}{2}$	$4\frac{3}{4} + \frac{3}{4}$	$8\frac{1}{2} + 4\frac{3}{4}$	$8\frac{1}{2} - \frac{3}{4}$

3 If we collected $\frac{1}{4}$ of a dollar for 80 days, how much money would we have?

4 If you read for $\frac{3}{4}$ hour per day, how many days would it take before you had spent 12 hours reading?

67

NAME _____ | DATE _____

 ## Barbara's Banana Bread Problems

Barbara has the following recipe for banana bread. The recipe makes 4 mini-loaves, 2 medium loaves, or 1 large loaf of bread. Barbara wants to make 50 mini-loaves.

1 cup sugar	$\frac{1}{2}$ cup shortening	2 eggs	3 bananas
$1\frac{3}{4}$ cups flour	1 teaspoon baking soda	$\frac{1}{2}$ teaspoon salt	$\frac{3}{4}$ cup nuts, optional

1 The first problem I am posing about this situation is:

2 Use this space to solve the problem and record your thinking with numbers, words, equations or models.

3 My solution:

4 The second problem I am posing about this situation is:

5 Use this space to solve the problem and record your thinking with numbers, words, equations or models.

6 My solution:

68

Edwin's Eggless Sugar Cookies Problems

1 Edwin usually makes 20 cookies with this recipe, but only wants 5 cookies.

1 stick butter $\frac{1}{2}$ cup sugar $\frac{1}{2}$ teaspoon vanilla 3 tablespoons milk

$1\frac{1}{2}$ cups flour 2 teaspoon baking powder $\frac{1}{4}$ teaspoon salt

a The problem I am posing about this situation is:

b Use this space to solve the problem and record your thinking with numbers, words, equations or models.

c My solution:

2 Roberta wants to use Edwin's recipe to make lots of cookies. She has:

6 sticks butter 3 cups sugar 4 teaspoon vanilla 20 tablespoons milk

7 cups flour 10 teaspoons baking powder 2 teaspoons salt

a The problem I am posing about this situation is:

b Use this space to solve the problem and record your thinking with numbers, words, equations or models.

c My solution:

Meadow Grid

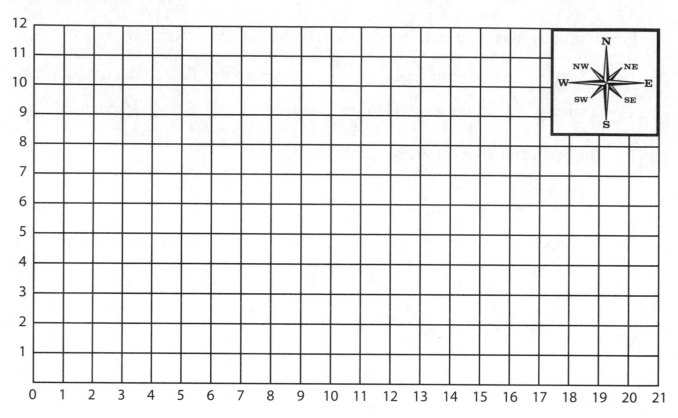

Nest 1	Nest 2	Nest 3	Nest 4	Nest 5
F.A. 1A	F.A. 2A	F.A. 3A	F.A. 4A	F.A. 5A
F.A. 1B	F.A. 2B	F.A. 3B	F.A. 4B	F.A. 5B

Nest 6	Nest 7	Nest 8	Nest 9	Nest 10
F.A. 6A	F.A. 7A	F.A. 8A	F.A. 9A	F.A. 10A
F.A. 6B	F.A. 7B	F.A. 8B	F.A. 9B	F.A. 10B

70

Mole Building Codes

Although Mumford Mole is a fictional character, it's really true that moles spend most of their lives underground and are skilled tunnelers. Many people think moles are big pests because they dig their tunnels everywhere, including lawns and gardens. Most types of moles don't eat the plants, though. What they're after are worms and insects, including insects that damage people's lawns, gardens, and plants. Moles also make the soil healthier because their tunnels let air and water go deeper into the dirt.

Use this page to list as many observations as you can about the tunneling rules Mumford learned from Old Emeritus Mole. What kinds of patterns can you detect in Mumford's work? If you look carefully enough, you'll find there are certain things he always does.

Mole Facts:

- There are about 30 different kinds of moles around the world. The United States is home to 7 of these types, including the coast mole, the star-nosed mole, and the eastern mole. (Mumford Mole is an eastern mole.)

- Moles eat earthworms, grubs, beetles, ants, and other insect larvae. They usually eat more than their own weight in food every day.

- Moles can tunnel up to 12–15 feet an hour!

Another Mole Map

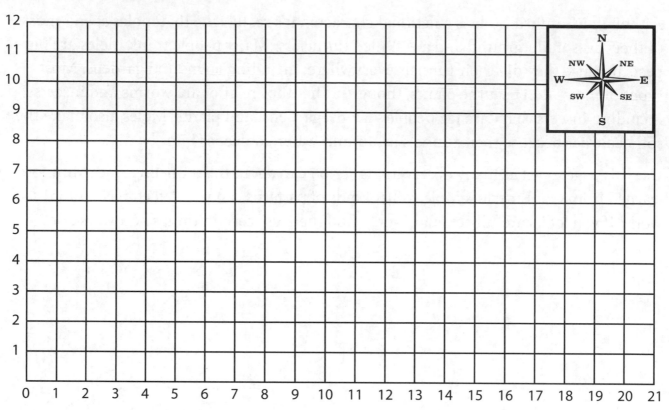

1   Plot the points listed and label each on the coordinate grid.

Nests: Feeding Areas:

N1 (3, 3)   FA 1a (1, 5)

N2 (13, 11)   FA 1b (5, 5)

N3 (19, 3)   FA 2a (11, 9)

                        FA 2b (15, 9)

                        FA 3a (17, 5)

                        FA 3b (17, 1)

2   If each space on the coordinate grid represents one yard, how many feet apart are:

a   Nest 1 and Nest 3?

b   Feeding Areas 1b and 3a?

c   Feeding Areas 2a and 2b?

Fluid Ounces Conversions

| quart | cup | gallon | pint | fluid ounce |

1 Look at the pictures above that show some of the customary units we use to measure liquid volume. In the spaces below, write the units in order from smallest to largest.

2 Use the table below to record the equivalencies for the Two Quarts or Spill Spinner.

Amount	Convert to Fluid Ounces
1 cup	
$\frac{1}{2}$ cup	
$\frac{1}{4}$ cup	
$\frac{3}{4}$ cup	
$1\frac{1}{4}$ cups	

Amount	Convert to Fluid Ounces	Convert to Cups
$1\frac{3}{4}$ cups		
2 cups		
1 pint		
1 quart		
1 gallon		

3 Use the information in the table above to answer the following questions.

How many pints are equal to a gallon?	How many quarts are equal to a gallon?
How many pints are equal to a quart?	How many cups are equal to a quart?

4 Write some comparisons between units here.

a _____ are equal to _____.

b _____ are equal to _____.

c _____ are equal to _____.

Fraction Splat! Game 1

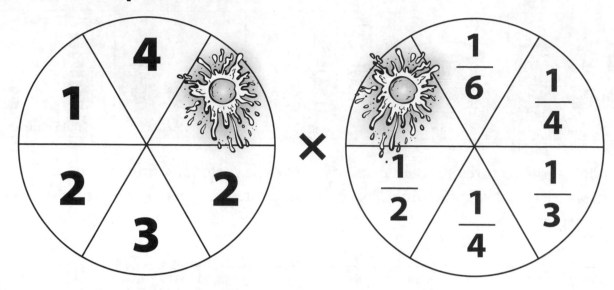

This game we will play for a low/high score.

Team 1					
	Turn 1	**Turn 2**	**Turn 3**	**Turn 4**	**Round Total**	**Work**
Round 1						
Round 2						
				Game Total		

Team 2					
	Turn 1	**Turn 2**	**Turn 3**	**Turn 4**	**Round Total**	**Work**
Round 1						
Round 2						
				Game Total		

Team _____ won by _____ points.

NAME _____ | **DATE** _____

Fraction Splat! Game 2

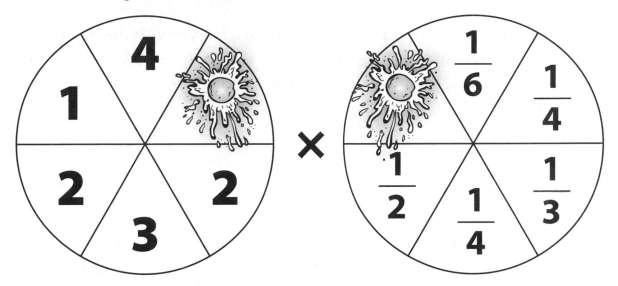

This game we will play for a low/high score.

Team 1					
	Turn 1	**Turn 2**	**Turn 3**	**Turn 4**	**Round Total**	**Work**
Round 1						
Round 2						
				Game Total		

Team 2					
	Turn 1	**Turn 2**	**Turn 3**	**Turn 4**	**Round Total**	**Work**
Round 1						
Round 2						
				Game Total		

Team _____ won by _____ points.

May Problems

1   Craig did an hour of yardwork after school for 8 days in a row. At the end of the 8 days, his mom gave him $40.00, which included a bonus of $8.00 for sticking to the schedule and working carefully. How much did he earn each day, not including the bonus money?

2   Whitney's dance class starts at 4:30 p.m. Next Tuesday, she wants to get there 15 minutes early to practice a new routine with her friends. It takes her 25 minutes to get ready and 10 minutes to get there. What time should Whitney start getting ready?

3   Gemma got a box of beads for her birthday. When she opened the box, she saw that there were 3 more white beads than red beads. There were half as many red beads as blue beads. There were one–third as many blue beads as purple beads. There were 12 purple beads. How many beads were in the box?

4   Nick's dad accidentally dropped the cookie jar, and half the cookies fell on the floor and had to be thrown away. While he was cleaning up the mess, the dog got into the cookie jar and ate two-thirds of the cookies that were left. Then Nick's little brother snuck in and ate half of the cookies that were still left. When Nick's dad finally got done cleaning up the mess, there were only 4 cookies left in the jar. How many cookies were there to start with?

Problem String Work Space

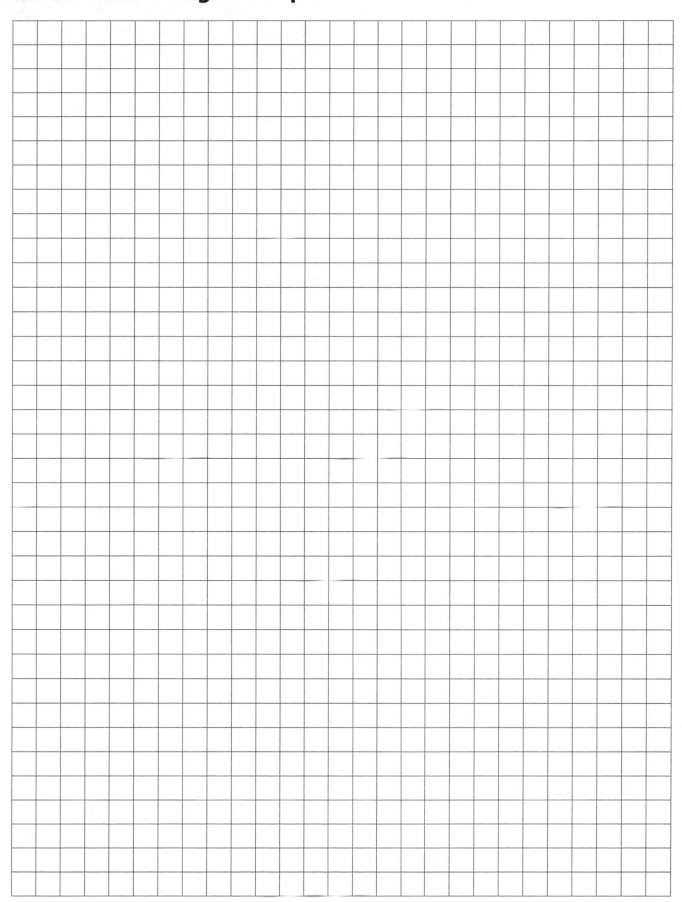

A1

Problem String Work Space

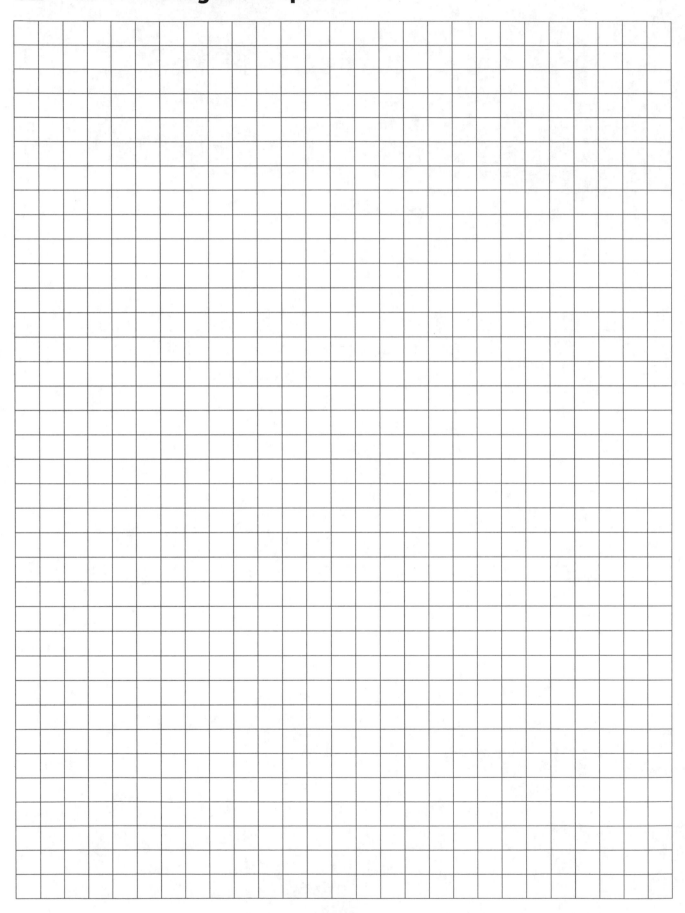

A2

Problem String Work Space

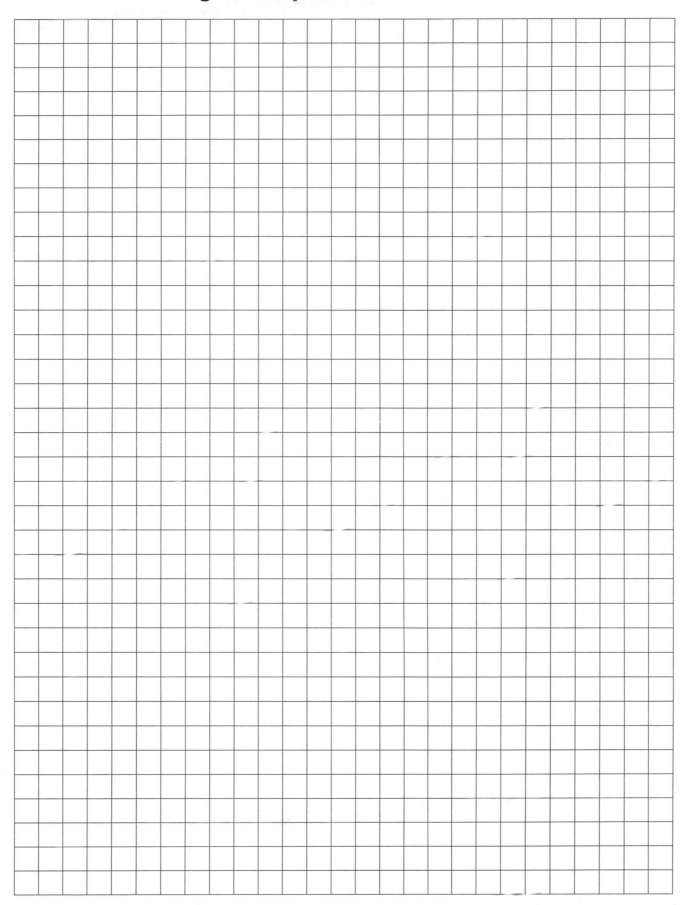

Problem String Work Space

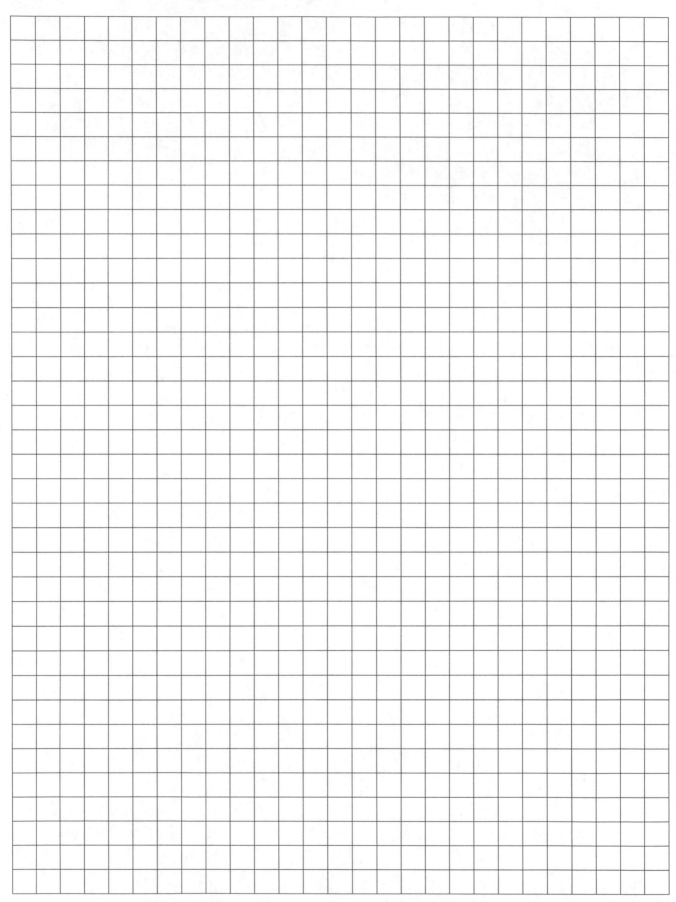

Problem String Work Space

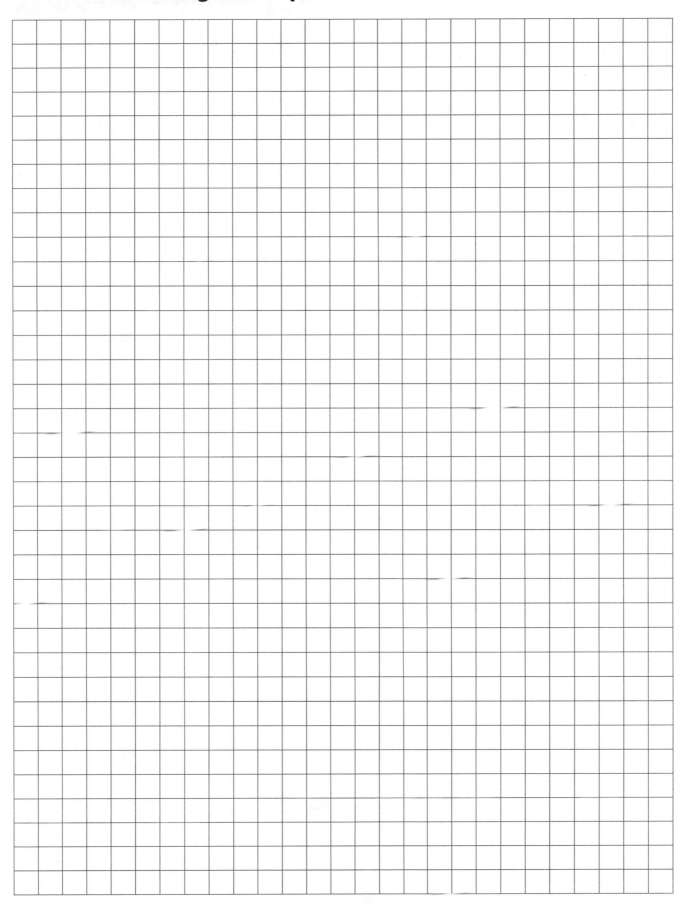

A5

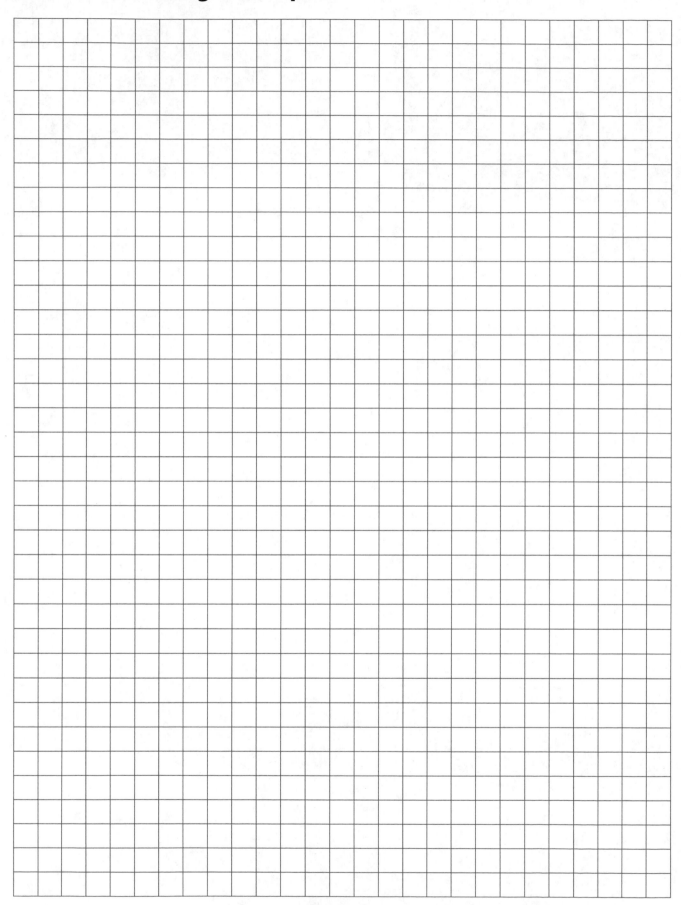 Problem String Work Space

Problem String Work Space

Problem String Work Space

Problem String Work Space

Problem String Work Space

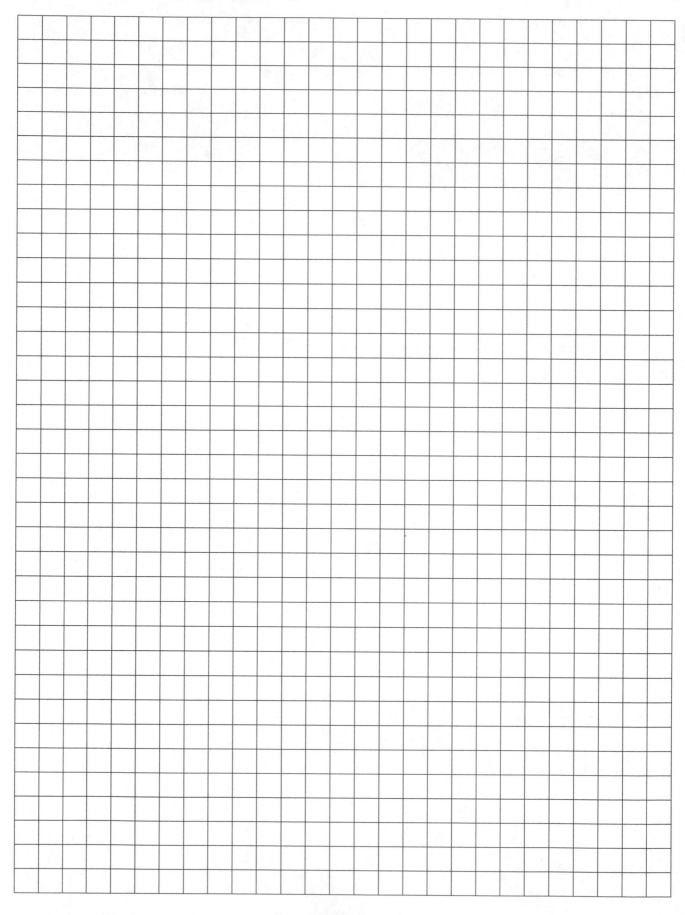

Problem String Work Space

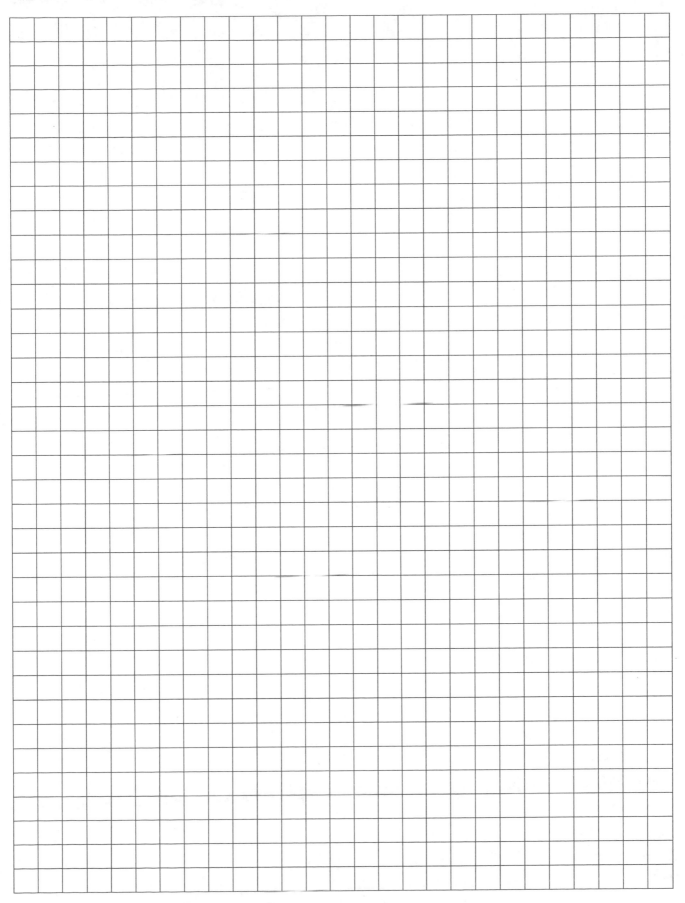

Problem String Work Space

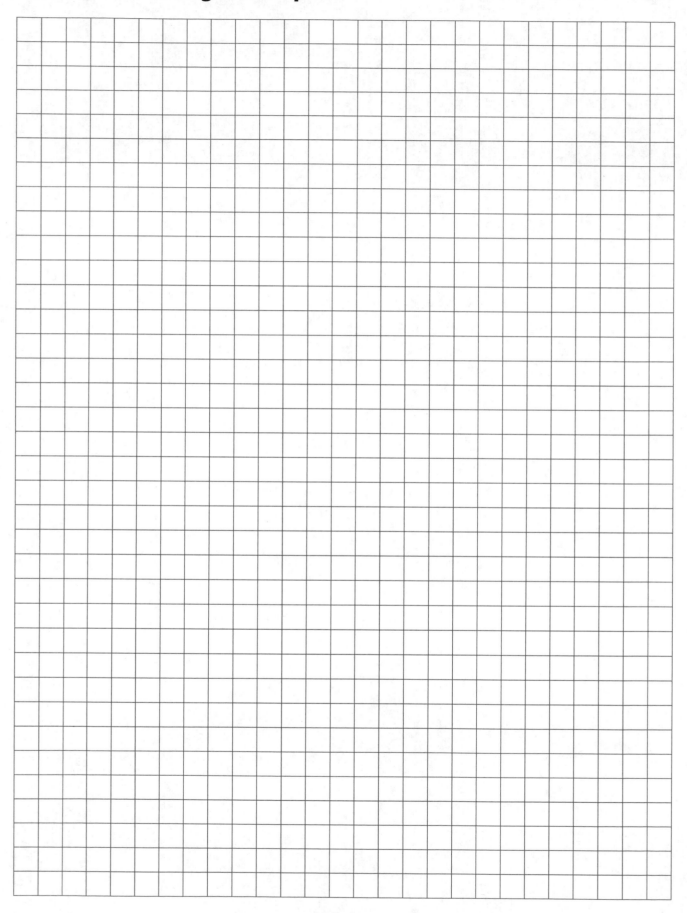

A12

Problem String Work Space

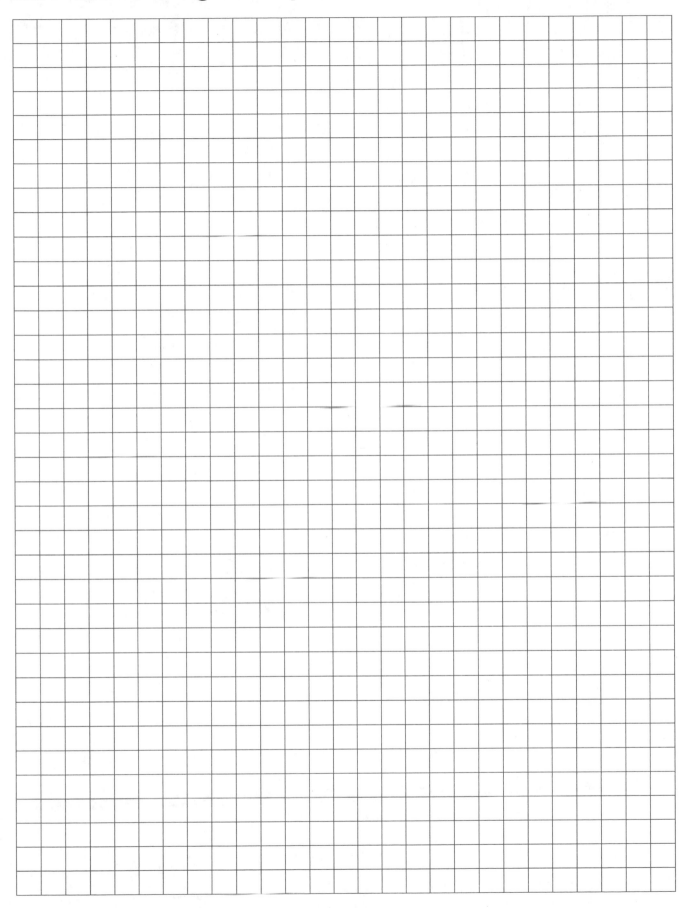

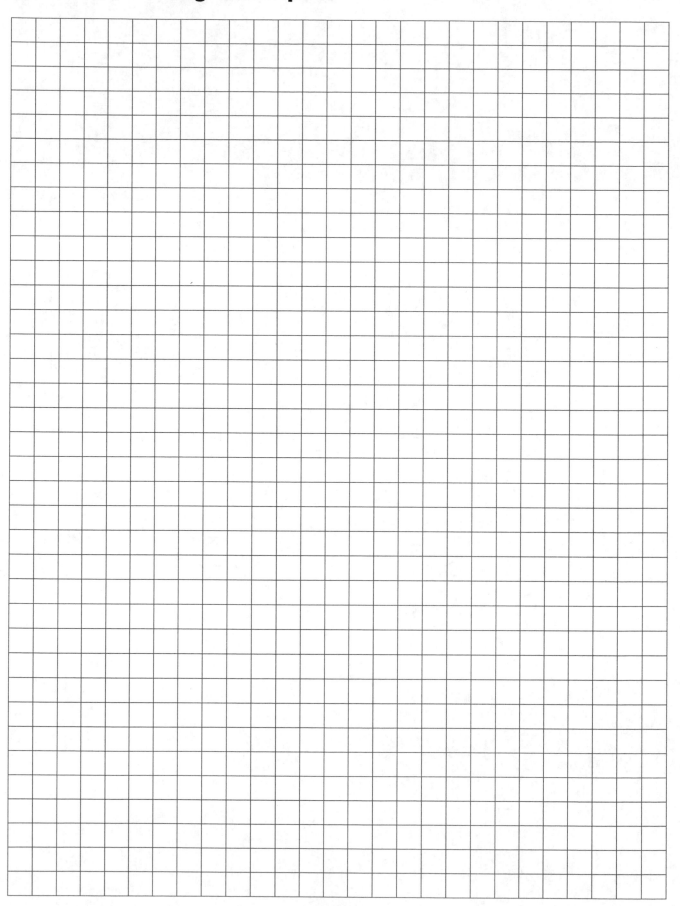 Problem String Work Space

Problem String Work Space

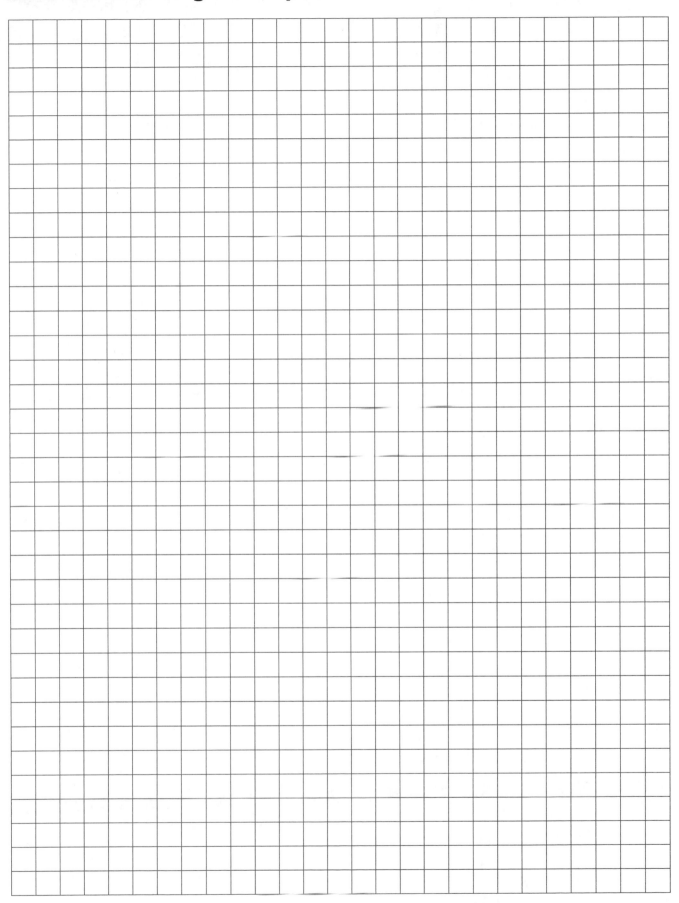

A15

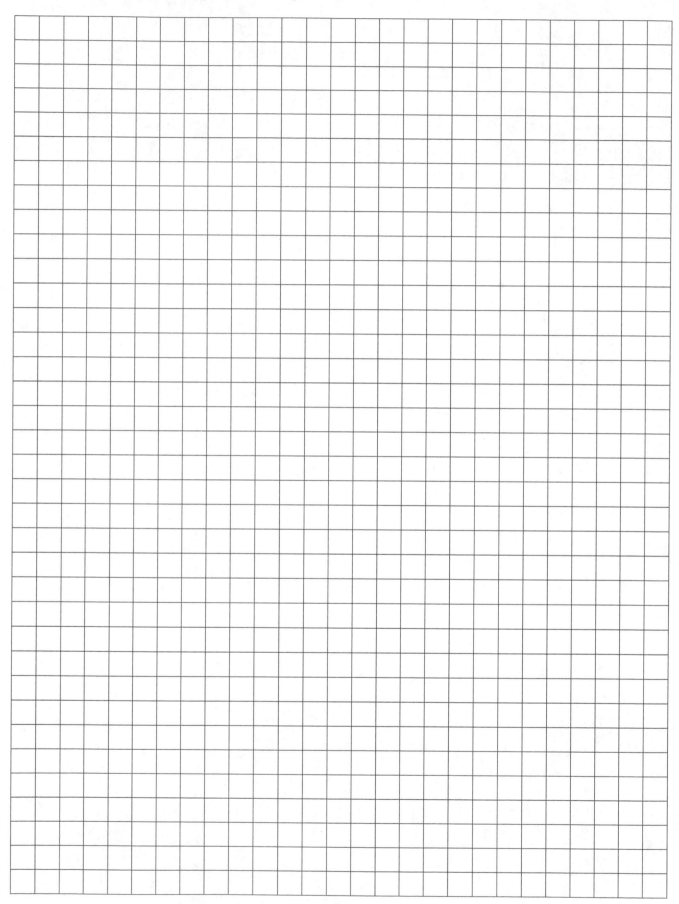

Problem String Work Space

Problem String Work Space

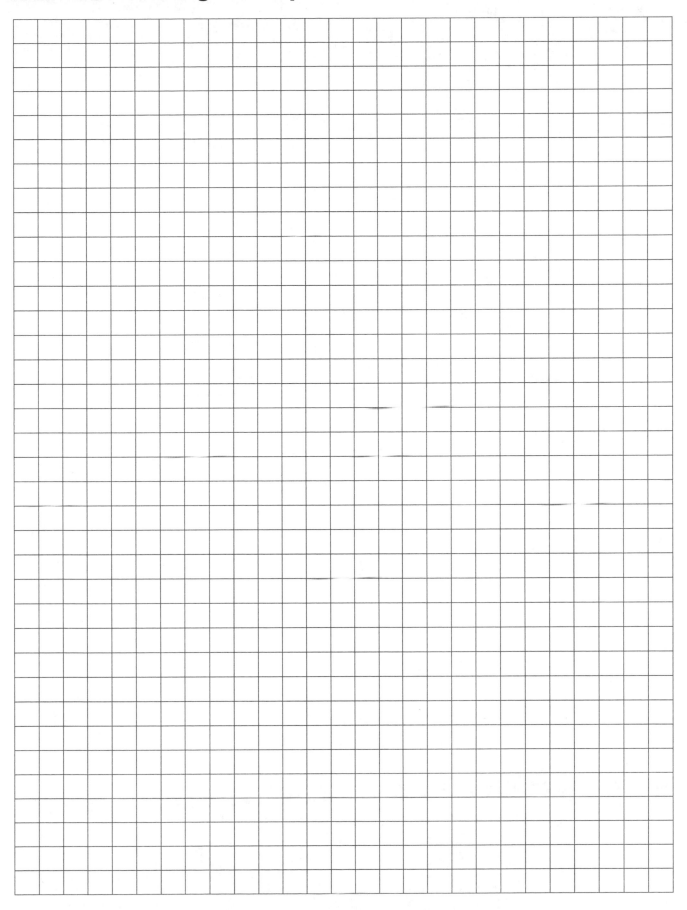

Problem String Work Space

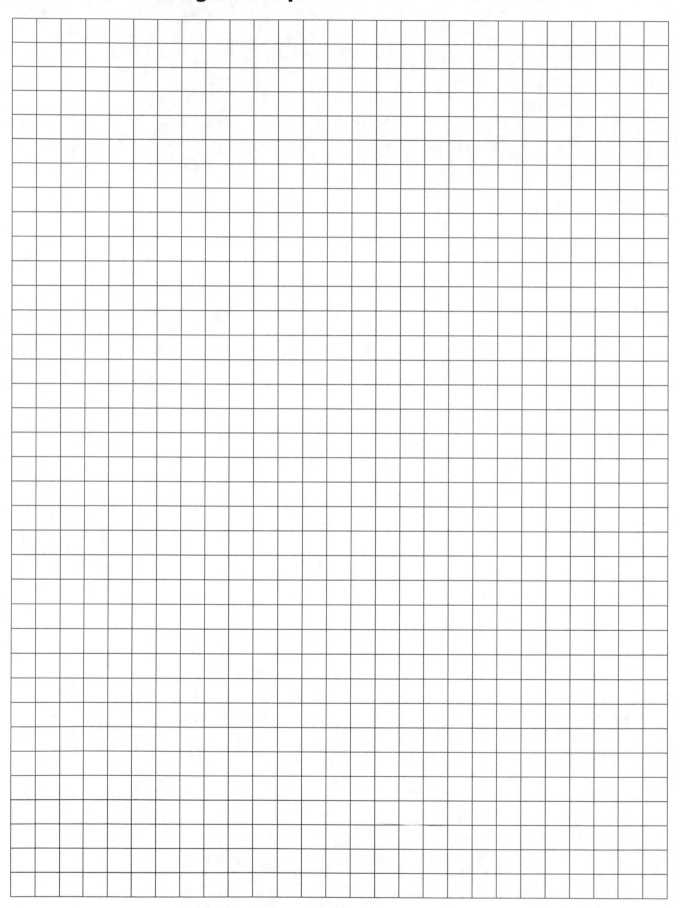

Problem String Work Space

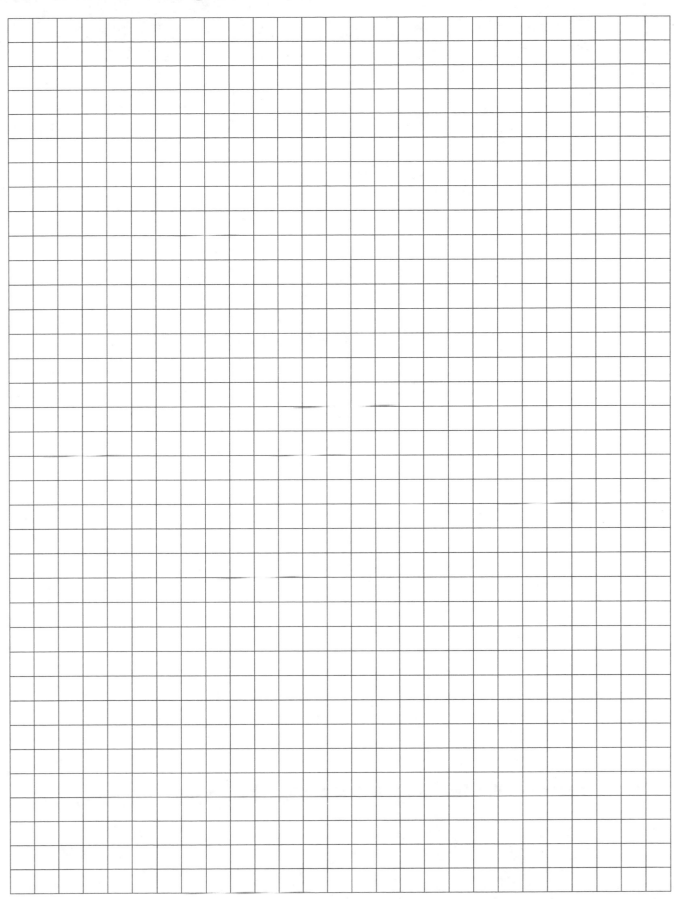

A19

Problem String Work Space

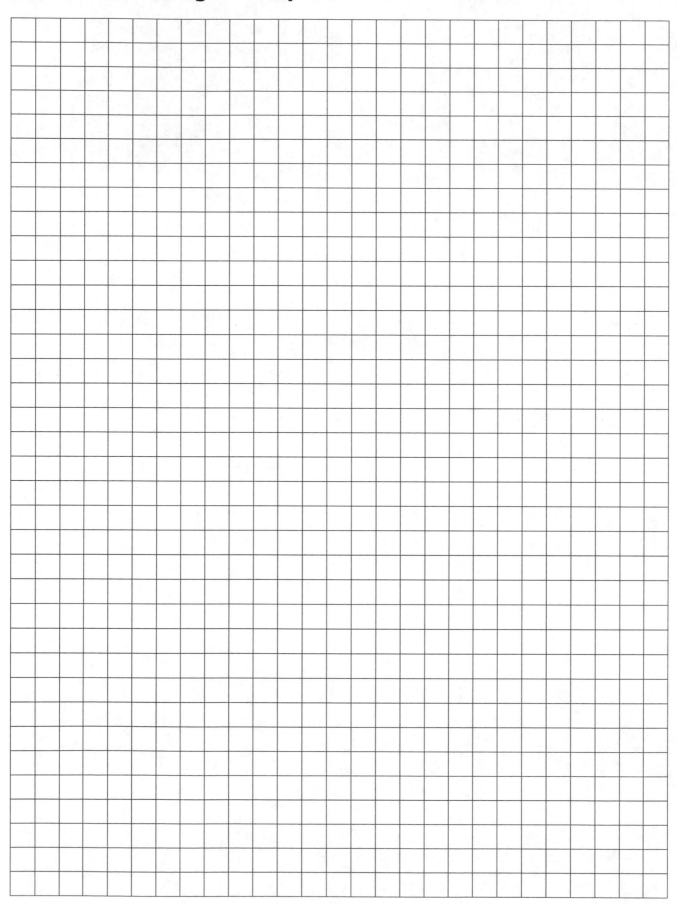

Problem String Work Space

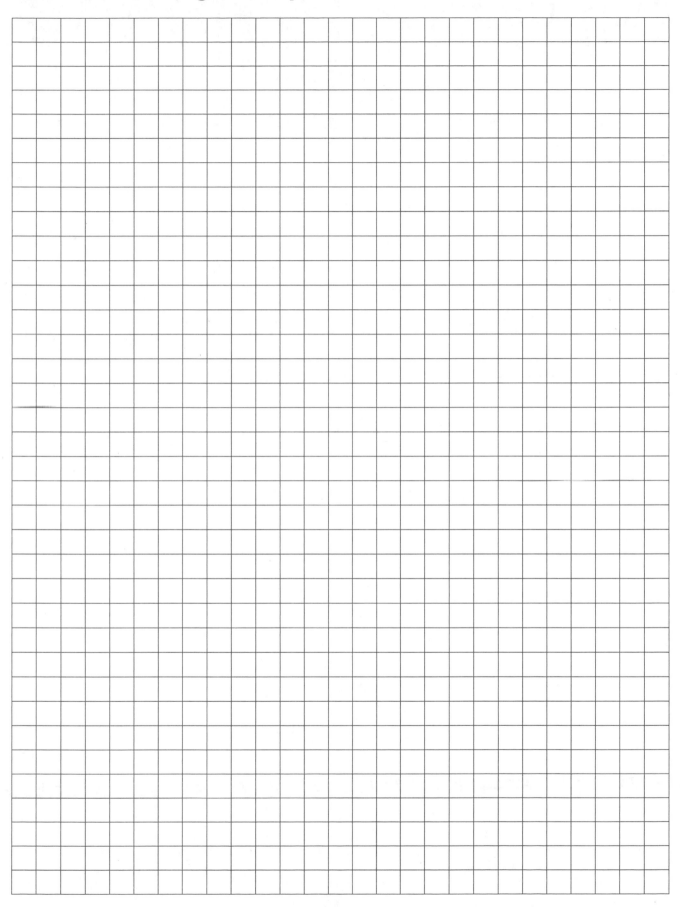

Problem String Work Space

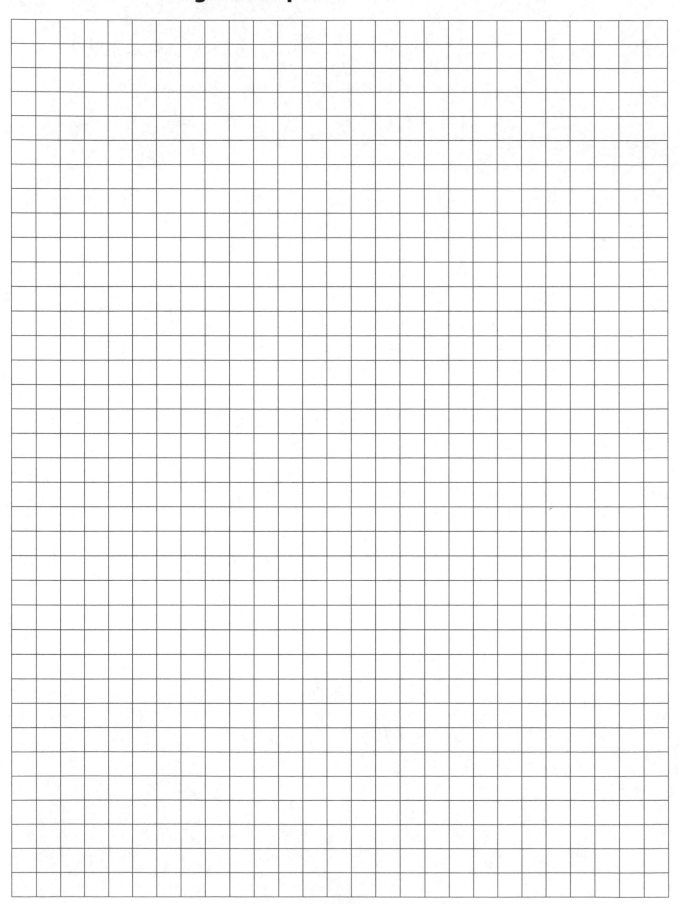

Problem String Work Space

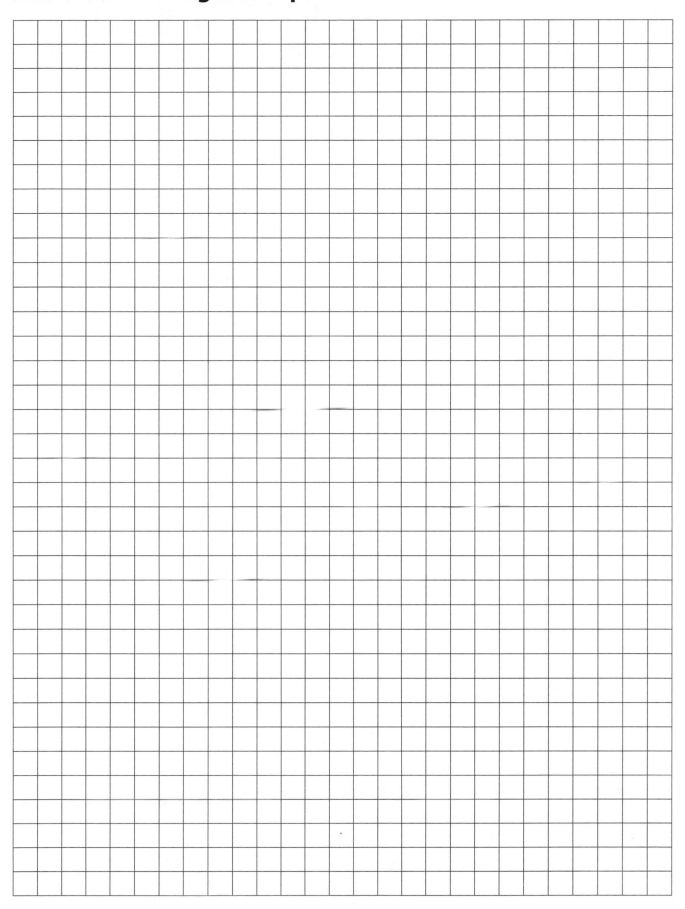

A23

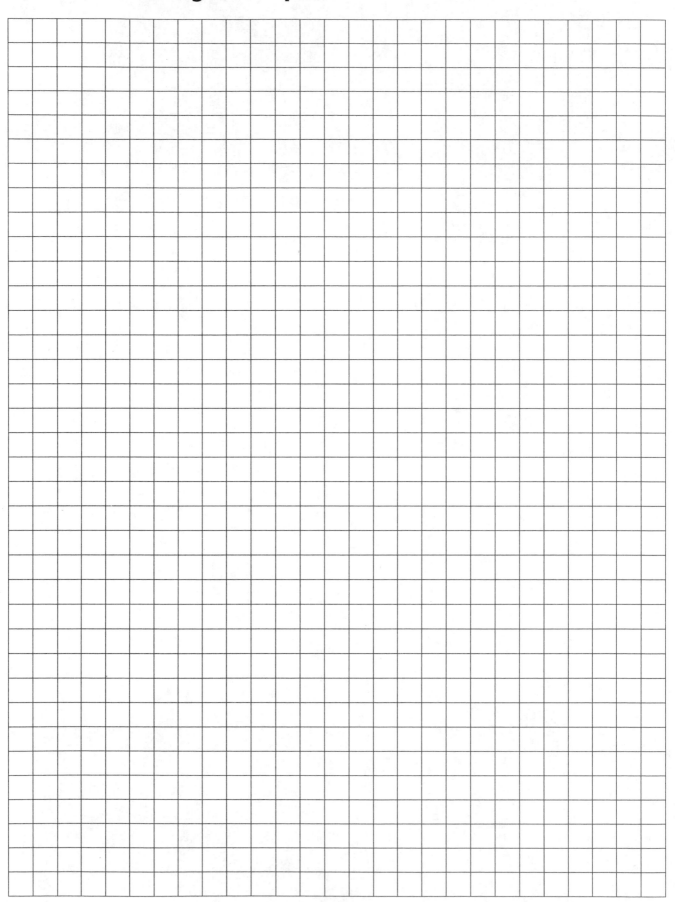 Problem String Work Space

Problem String Work Space

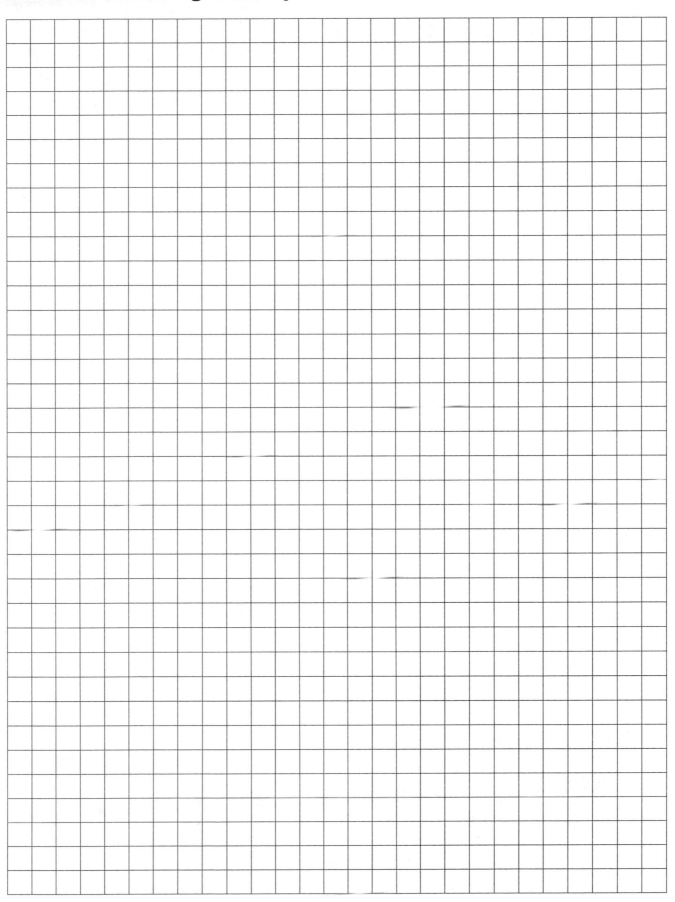

 Problem String Work Space

Problem String Work Space

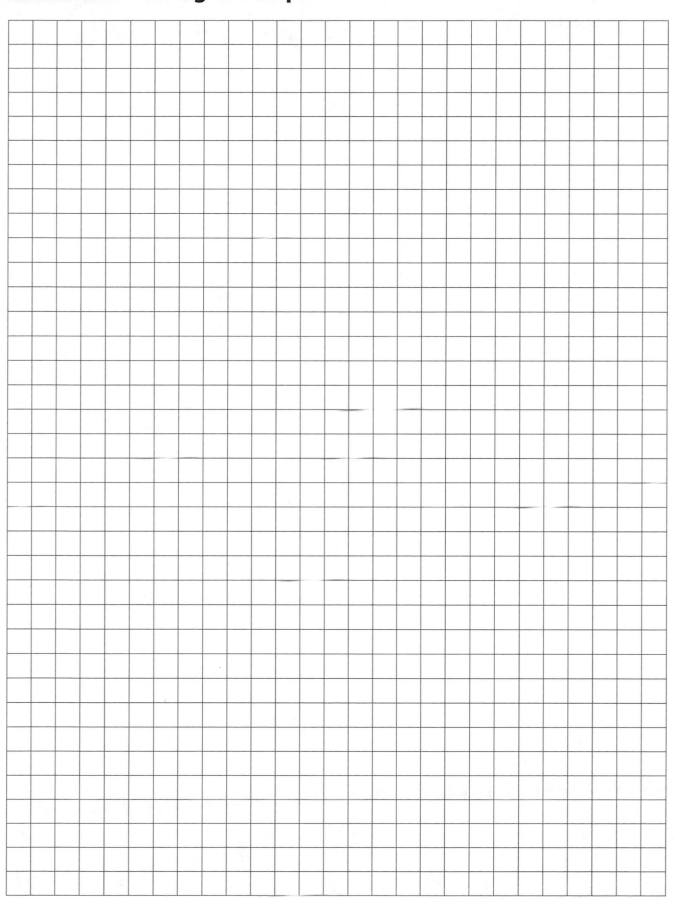

A27

Problem String Work Space

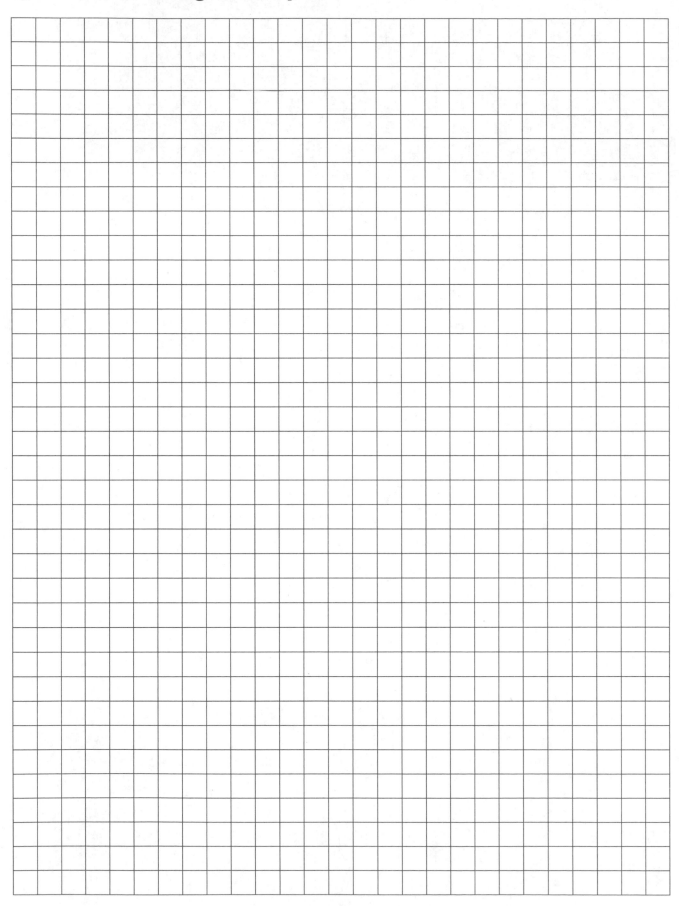

Problem String Work Space

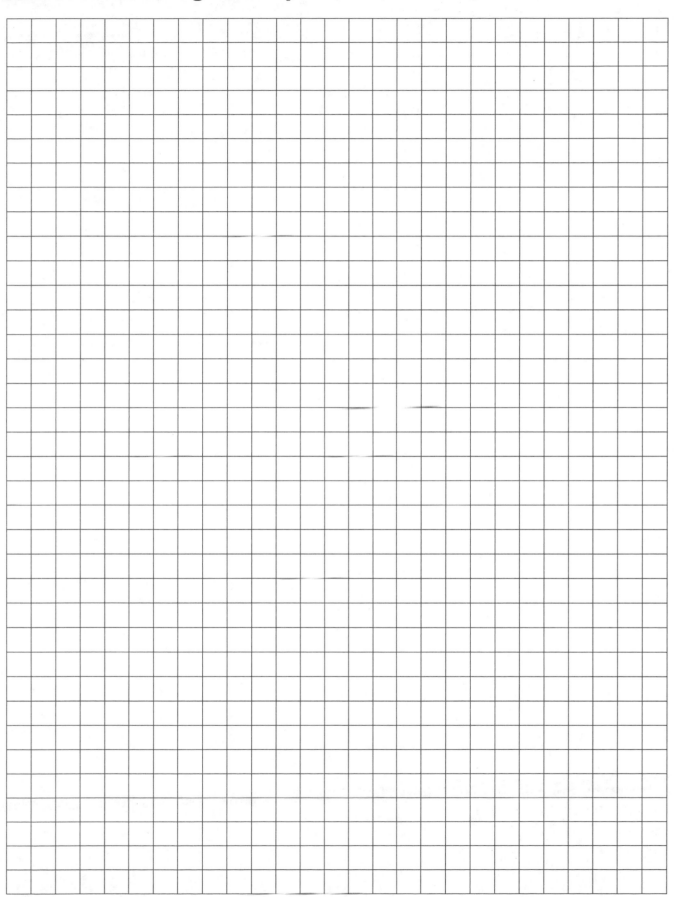

A29

Problem String Work Space

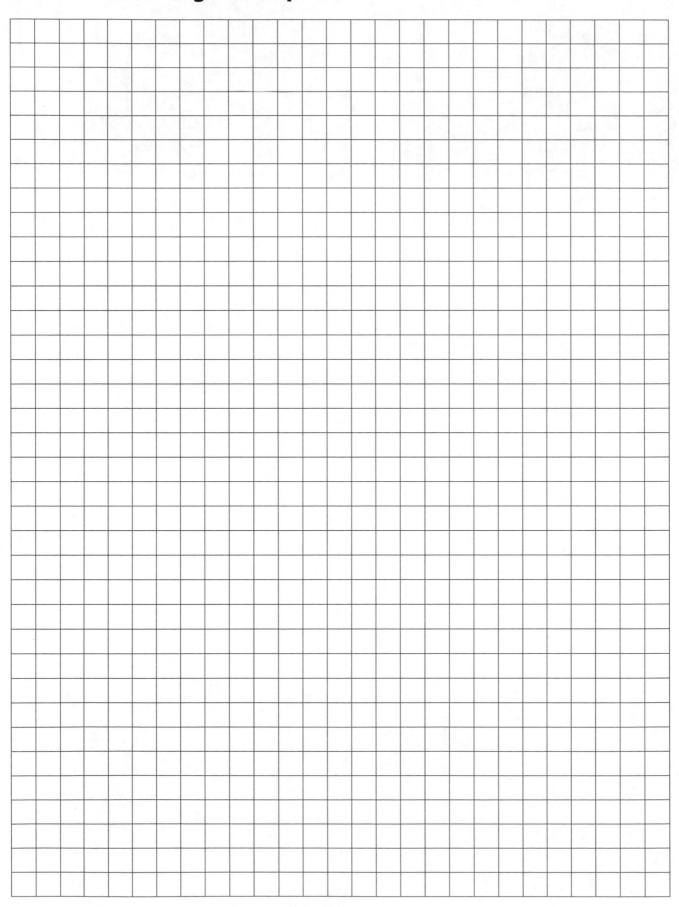

Problem String Work Space

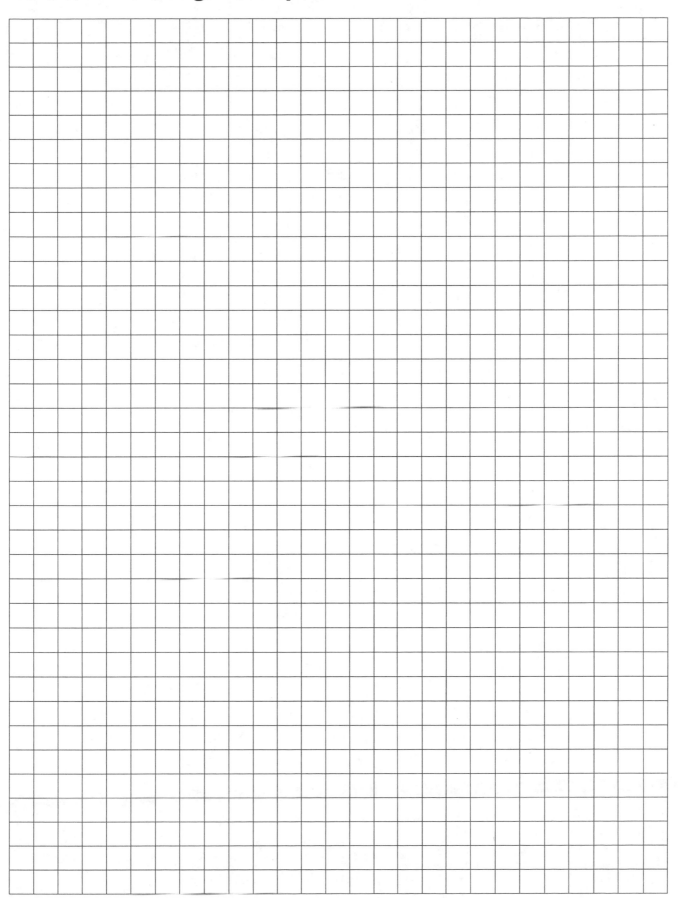

A31

Problem String Work Space

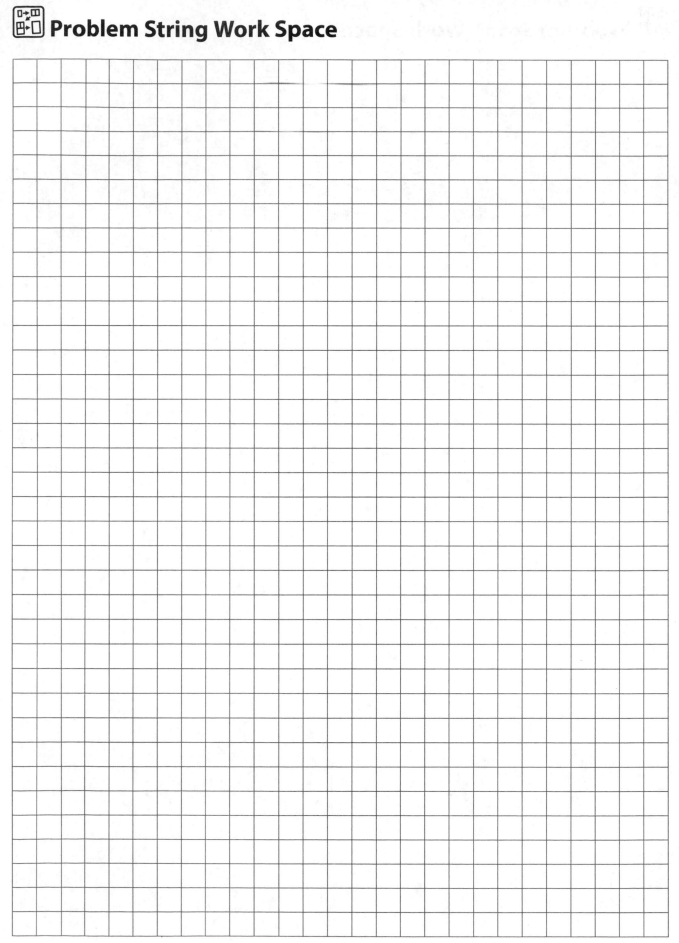